A Concise History of 20th Century Music

MB98567

By Graham Hearn

BILL'S MUSIC SHELF

© 2010 BY MEL BAY PUBLICATIONS, INC., PACIFIC, MO 63069.
ALL RIGHTS RESERVED. INTERNATIONAL COPYRIGHT SECURED. B.M.I. MADE AND PRINTED IN U.S.A.
No part of this publication may be reproduced in whole or in part, or stored in a retrieval system, or transmitted in any form or by any means, electronic, mechanical, photocopy, recording, or otherwise, without written permission of the publisher.

Visit us on the Web at www.melbay.com or billsmusicshelf.com

Graham Hearn studied at Trinity College of Music, London, obtaining an external B.Mus from Durham University and at the University of York, gaining a D.Phil in composition, the first person in the United Kingdom to do so. Since the 1970s he has pursued a busy dual career as lecturer at Leeds College of Music, Britain's largest music conservatory, and freelance jazz pianist/arranger/composer. In his educational work he specialises in twentieth century music history and jazz composition and conducting the New Music Ensemble.

He lives in Knaresborough, North Yorkshire, England, from where he can indulge his passions for walking, photography and bird-watching.

To Jill

Contents

List of Illustrations vii
Foreword ix
Preface x
Acknowledgements xi

PART 1: UP TO 1945

1 THE BEGINNINGS 15
Austro-Germany: Mahler and Strauss 17; France: Satie and Debussy 19; Free Atonality 24; Problems of Form 26; Emancipation Continues 27; New Aspects of Timbre 28; Rhythm 29; Stravinsky's Later Russian Works 33; Seeds of Change 34; Varèse 35

2 NATIONALISM, FOLK MUSIC, EXOTICISM 39
Bartók 39; England 42; Janáček 47; Spain 47; Popular Culture 49; The Exotic 51; South America 52; The Spirit of Independence – Ives and Cowell 53

3 SERIALISM 59
Schoenberg, Berg and Webern 59; The early work of John Cage 62

4 NEO-CLASSICISM 67
Ravel 68; Stravinsky 70; Les Six 73; Music of Social Conscience 76; Weill 79; Russia 80; America 81; Sibelius and Nielsen 84

PART 2: AFTER 1945

1 A FRESH BEGINNING 89
Messiaen 90; Messiaen's Influence 94; Integral Serialism 95; Boulez and Stockhausen 96; Musique Concrète and Electronic Music 100; The Darmstadt Legacy 103; Theater 105; Music Theater in England 107; The Middle Ages Revisited 108; Indeterminacy, Chance and Aleatoricism 110; Reactions 119; Experimentalism 122; Groups 123; English Experimental Music 123; The Spirit of Independence Continued 127; Nancarrow 130; Texture 132

2	**MINIMALISM**	**135**
3	**POST-MINIMALISM**	**147**
	Adams, Torke, Bang on a Can 147; Totalism 150; Andriessen and Martland 150; Pärt and Others 151	
4	**RESPONSES**	**155**
	Tippett, Carter, Stravinsky 155; New Complexity 156; Xenakis 158; Spectralism 159	
5	**PIONEERS COME OF AGE**	**163**
	Later Feldman 163; Later Cage 164; Later Stockhausen 165; Revisions 166	
6	**OTHER RESPONSES**	**171**
	Lachenmann 171; Scelsi 172; Younger Germanic Composers 173	
7	**REFERENCE AND QUOTATION**	**177**
8	**OTHER CURRENTS**	**187**
	Macmillan, Turnage 187; Further uses of Jazz 189; Ruders 190; Conservatives 191; Younger English Composers 198	
9	**WINDS FROM THE EAST**	**201**
	Australia 205	
10	**THE CRISIS OF CONTEMPORARY MUSIC**	**207**
	Notes	209
	Suggested Further Reading	212
	Index	215

Illustrations

Gustav Mahler	18
Erik Satie	22
Claude Debussy	23
Schoenberg and His School	25
Igor Stravinsky	30
Edgard Varèse	35
Béla Bartók	40
Ralph Vaughan Williams	44
Manuel de Falla	48
Charles Ives	54
Henry Cowell	56
Maurice Ravel	68
Benjamin Britten	77
Michael Tippett	78
Dmitri Shostakovich	81
Olivier Messiaen	96
Pierre Boulez, Karlheinz Stockhausen	97
Pierre Henry	101
Luciano Berio	104
Peter Maxwell Davies, Harrison Birtwistle	107
John Cage	111
Morton Feldman	115
Hans Werner Henze	120
Harry Partch	127
Conlon Nancarrow	130
György Ligeti	132
LaMonte Young	136
Steve Reich and Graham Hearn	139
Philip Glass	143
Arvo Pärt	151
Kaija Saariaho	160
George Benjamin	161
Robin Holloway	180
Mauricio Kagel	183

Illustrations

Mark-Anthony Turnage		188
Poul Ruders		191
David Matthews		193
Unsuk Chin		202
Tōru Takemitsu		203

Examples:

1	Satie, Ogive No.2	20
2	Mahler, Symphony No.10. 1st movement, bar 206	24
3	Stravinsky, The Rite of Spring ('Augurs of Spring'); bitonal chord	32
4	Bartók String Quartet No.4, fifth movement, opening	41
5	Vaughan Williams, Symphony No.5, first movement, opening theme	44
6	Vaughan Williams, 'The Captain's Apprentice' (Norfolk Rhapsody)	45
7	Berg, Violin Concerto (note row)	60
8	Webern, Concerto Op.24 (note row)	62
9	Stravinsky, Symphony in C (coda to last movement)	72
10(a)	Messiaen, Second mode of limited transposition	91
10(b)	Messiaen, Characteristic chords derived from 2nd mode	91
11	Messiaen, Couleurs de la cité céleste (fig.18)	93
12	Stockhausen, Piano Piece 1, bar 53	99
13	Wolff, For 1, 2 or 3 People	113
14	Brown, December 1952 (from *Folio*)	114
15	Feldman, Intersection II, bars 130–258	115
16	Cage, Fontana Mix, sample superimposition of materials.	117
17	Lutosławski, Jeux vénétiens, 12-note chord	119
18	Penderecki, Tren. p.8	134
19	Reich, Electric Counterpoint, Chord progression, measures 1–8	144
20	Gordon, Trance, measures 532-535	149
21	Ferneyhough, Unity Capsule, p.14	157
22	Schnittke, Stille Nacht, fig 2	182
23	Britten, Strange Meeting (War Requiem), fig 121	195

Foreword

Graham Hearn, composer, jazz pianist, arranger, conductor and educator, has written a deeply informative, enthusiastic and perceptive guide to twentieth century music. Drawing on his immense experience as a professional musician, conducting hundreds of performances of contemporary compositions and as a virtuoso jazz artist, he has provided an invaluable introduction to the complexities of twentieth century musical history.

We would like to express our gratitude to William Bay and all his staff at Mel Bay Publications Inc. for making this book possible and to Elizabeth Wade for her patient and dedicated editorial assistance during the preparation of this work.

Graham Wade
General Editor

PREFACE

This book is intended as a comprehensive survey and concise reference book of twentieth century music for both students in schools and colleges and the general public. My aim has been to highlight where composers have pushed boundaries, stretched our credibility and shown such leaps of imagination as to make us remember that the twentieth century is possibly the most extraordinary of them all. If this can stimulate the reader to enquire and listen further, then my job is done.

Thanks are due to Jo Dawson at Boosey & Hawkes, London; Bettina Tiefenbrunner at Universal Edition, Vienna; Eric Forder at Schott/Universal in London; Tim Brooke at Faber & Faber, London and my friend Bill Kinghorn (a fine but tragically unsung composer) for the loan of scores and other materials. My thanks also to Elizabeth North for much helpful advice and Mark Donlon for technical assistance with computers; to my editors, Elizabeth and Graham Wade for their expertise and patience, and to my partner, Jill Jackson, to whom this book is gratefully dedicated.

Graham Hearn,
YORKSHIRE, ENGLAND, 2009

ACKNOWLEDGEMENTS

Grateful acknowledgments are due to the following publishing houses for granting permission to quote from the works listed:

BOOSEY & HAWKES: Britten; War Requiem: Reich; Electric Counterpoint: Schnittke; Stille Nacht: Stravinsky; The Rite of Spring.

DESHON MUSIC INC: Penderecki; Threnody for the Victims of Hiroshima.

MANNHEIMER MUSIKVERLAG MÜNCHEN: Lutosławski; Venetian Games.

MUSIC SALES: Brown; December 1952 (AMP): Gordon; Trance (Red Poppy).

OXFORD UNIVERSITY PRESS: Vaughan Williams; Symphony No. 5 and Norfolk Rhapsody No. 1.

PETERS EDITION LIMITED: Cage; Fontana Mix: Feldman; Intersection 2: Ferneyhough; Unity Capsule: Wolff; For 1, 2 or 3 People.

SCHOTT MUSIC LTD: Stravinsky; Symphony in C.

UNITED MUSIC PUBLISHERS: Messiaen; Couleurs de la Cité Céleste and Technique of my Musical Language (Leduc): Satie; Ogives No.2 (Chant du Monde).

UNIVERSAL EDITION: Bartók; String Quartet No. 4: Stockhausen; Piano Piece 1: Webern; Concerto Op.24.

PART 1:
UP TO *1945*

1
THE BEGINNINGS

THE MOST NOTICEABLE FEATURES OF music in the twentieth century, surely familiar to anyone who has sampled even the smallest amount, have been its bewildering variety, its frequent complexity and its rapid rate of change, so that one cannot talk of "*a* twentieth century style." The several styles which constitute the vast panorama of twentieth century music vary in their degree of distance from the music of the past, and though many of them share certain characteristics, there are also some striking differences.

The year 1928, for example, saw the appearance of Bartók's Hungarian folksong-inspired **Fourth String Quartet**, Webern's austere and abstract **Symphony** and Weill's **Threepenny Opera**, with its strong flavors of the Berlin cabaret. Thirty years later, in 1958, the situation had hardly changed, though the range of diversification certainly had, for in that year Messiaen completed the last instalments of his **Catalogue d'oiseaux**, an epic celebration of birdsong, Britten wrote his **Nocturne**, an atmospheric, tonal song-cycle, and Cage produced one of his most complex graphic scores, **Fontana Mix**. This is both curious and fascinating; all these works seem to inhabit different worlds yet they can be placed unequivocally in the twentieth century. The reasons for this apparent chaos are complex and varied, but it is clear that, in the century or so following the watershed of the French Revolution, the Western world witnessed the gradual deterioration of the hegemony of Church and State and the dissipation of their patronage through the spread of nationalism, the rise of democracy and the cult of the individual. Later on came the opening up of the outside world through the discovery of exotic cultures, and the inner world through the exploration of the subconscious, as well as the steady advance of technology.

The effect of all this on composers was to encourage them to pursue a greater individuality and to experiment with the language of music, expanding its resources to accommodate a wider expressive range. At the same time, a parallel mistrust of the new values elicited the opposite: a maintenance of the belief in the continuing viability of the old established techniques, seen in the survival well into the twentieth century of quite traditional approaches to tonality.

This had even further, and more serious, repercussions in the creation of a split between music-as-art and music-as-entertainment. Intriguingly, and perhaps confusingly, art music has been able to accommodate both radical and reactionary tendencies whereas entertainment music has eschewed the radical and kept faith with a relatively simple language, rooted in popular song and dance. Thus for the first time in its history, music became polarized into two distinct and separate entities, each with its own values and increasingly its own language.

We have already noted the ongoing fragmentation within art music. Entertainment (or popular) music has also shown a tendency to fragmentation but its basic function of appealing to the greatest number of people naturally precludes any radical experimentation with the language. It can spice up its harmony by borrowing from Ravel but cannot seriously entertain a similar borrowing from, say, Webern. Borrowing between categories and attempts at cross-over have always been, and still are, common, of course, but that does not deny the existence of the fundamental split described above and the functional differences therein.

AUSTRO-GERMANY: MAHLER AND STRAUSS

Both this split and the fragmentation within art music were well under way by the end of the nineteenth century, but Austro-German Romanticism was the dominating force and the seat of progressive tendencies, particularly in matters of harmony and tonal organization. The work of Richard Wagner (1813–83) is central to these developments and in his music drama **Tristan und Isolde** (completed in 1859) he demonstrated hitherto unheard-of possibilities of chromaticism, generating great swathes of ambiguous, unsettled harmony out of the expressive needs of the drama.

Wagner's friend, close colleague and eventual father-in-law Franz Liszt (1811–86) went even further with his almost obsessive use of the augmented triad and its associated whole tone scale, especially in his late works. All this was to have a far-reaching effect on later generations of composers wishing to build on Wagner's and Liszt's achievements, for the implications were nothing short of the complete disruption of tonality.

Richard Strauss (1864–1949), for example, satisfied the expressive needs of his first two operas, **Salome** (1905) and **Elektra** (1908), by an extensive use of unresolved dissonance and even bitonal harmonies. The process is also clearly seen in the symphonies of Gustav Mahler (1860–1911). These works contain a welter of innovation, both technical and expressive, which derives from the composer's belief in composition as autobiography. The expressive range runs the whole gamut from serenity to violence to anguish to hysteria, many of these conditions new to music and made possible by Mahler's exposure to the pioneering work in psychology of Freud and Jung in uncovering the workings of the subconscious. There are frequent references, too, to folk and popular music and Mahler's concern with the truthful portrayal of experience means that several of these elements may be placed in close proximity, to often devastating effect.

Mahler's enlargement of his emotional palette forced a corresponding expansion of his musical language, and in this he made some startling innovations: quartal harmonies, independent contrapuntal lines, unresolved dissonances, sudden and violent changes of key, wide displacement of notes in melodies and the breaking down of huge orchestral forces into small groups of unusual instrumentations. Inevitably, structure was blown up to vast proportions with serious consequences for tonal coherence. In fact, concentric tonal organization was largely abandoned. The **Ninth Symphony** (1909), for example, opens in D major but closes in Db major.

To abandon his language completely and step into the atonal chasm was, however, not possible for Mahler, as indeed it was not for Strauss, who felt obliged to temper the excesses of **Salome** and **Elektra** and return to a safer, warmer, yet still exceedingly lush, chromaticism. And there, in this prolonged romantic twilight, Strauss remained, right up until his last work, the **Four Last Songs** of 1949. The crucial next step had then to be taken by a younger generation.

FRANCE: SATIE AND DEBUSSY

The dominant position of Austro-German romantic music, particularly the colossal figure of Wagner, was something all composers had to come to terms with, but as early as the 1880s there were signs of an emerging new sensibility. Its *locus* was Paris, capital of a country which had never wholly been able to embrace German Romanticism, the weight of its classical past, reinforced by powerful conservative institutions like the Schola Cantorum, proving to be extremely durable. This did not prevent the flourishing of a Wagner cult, however, and it was also near impossible to escape the harmonic innovations for which he was responsible.

Gabriel Fauré (1845–1924) was one who remained impervious to Wagner, his brand of chromaticism being of a rather different kind – more French, one might say. Where Wagner's harmony is restless, wandering through many different tonal centers, Fauré's is allusive, creating suspense by the use of exquisitely subtle enharmonic devices and elliptical progressions while staying within the same tonal orbit. There is also an elegance and poise in Fauré's music, far removed from the overpowering expressiveness of Wagner. But what gives his music its peculiarly French character are the distinctive modal inflections, an inheritance of the Schola's conservatism.

The influence of modality is one of the key elements of the new sensibility referred to above, an early and remarkable example being the four **Ogives** for piano (1886), one of several works composed by a young Erik Satie (1866–1925). In these pieces, quasi-plainchant melodies are presented as, firstly, a single line, then "harmonised" by mostly parallel or near-parallel triads. Such "harmony" is, of course, not functional but, rather, coloristic and it gives the music an archaic quality, like a thickened organum. The opening of the second piece is shown in Example 1:

Ex.1 Satie, Ogive No.2

Reproduced by permission of Editions Le Chant Du Monde, Paris/Universal Music Publishers Ltd

    Although hardly influential, owing to their remaining in obscurity for years, the **Ogives** may have been known to Debussy (1862–1918), since an almost identical progression of parallel triads appears in the latter's **La cathédrale engloutie,** from his first book of piano **Préludes** (1909–10). However, parallel chord progressions are to be found in other French composers of the nineteenth century, one of the most notable being Chabrier (1841–94), a composer whose work was well known to both Debussy and Satie.

    Nevertheless, the **Ogives** remain unique in that parallel chords are almost the *only* type of harmonic structure used. This is a clear indication of the direction French music was taking and Satie proved to be a key figure. In the **Sarabandes** for piano (1887), the technique is one of juxtaposing short phrases (the shortest is a single isolated dominant ninth) containing sequences of unrelated triads, dominant sevenths and ninths, in an overall quasi-modal framework.

From the 1910s onwards, Satie produced several sets of short piano pieces, notorious for their humoristic, often absurd, titles and performance directions. (One such example is the comment "I have no tobacco. Luckily I don't smoke" which appears towards the end of the first piece, **d'Holothurie**, of the set called **Embryons desséchés** (Dried-up Embryos) from 1913.) The relatively clear-cut harmonies of his earlier pieces were abandoned in favor of a more ambiguous language, typically in two parts and oscillating between modality and tonality, each rather loosely defined. Repeating patterns are a feature and the general atmosphere is one of childlike simplicity.

Popular music idioms (circus, music-hall, ragtime), which were enjoying a tremendous vogue at this time, are a notable feature of Satie's ballet **Parade** (1917), as are the by now familiar short-winded, tonally ambiguous phrases repeated and strung together in place of thematic development. The *drame symphonique* **Socrate** (1919) is similarly constructed and Satie avoids any engagement with the characters by having the text sung in an unchanging plainchant style. The work is, nevertheless, extremely moving in its understated way, particularly at the end where Socrates' death is accompanied by a gradual slowing down of the pulse.

Throughout his composing career, Satie cultivated irony, humor, detachment and innocence, in a deliberate and provocative stand against not only Romanticism, but art in general (*"J'emmerde l'art"*, he once proclaimed) which was intended to keep him independent of the musical trends of his day, modernist or otherwise. However, Debussy, as well as younger French composers such as Ravel (1875–1937), Milhaud (1892–1974) and Poulenc (1899–1963) were touched by some aspect or other of his music, if not his aesthetic. He was the true fountainhead of French modernism.

Ornella Volta
Erik Satie

This is to take nothing away from the revolution being brought about simultaneously by Satie's younger contemporary Debussy, whose **Prélude à l'après-midi d'un faune** (1894) is sometimes credited as being the birth of modern music.[1]

Owing to its successful premiere as much as anything, the work's impact has been far greater than that of Satie's early piano pieces, its sensuality masking some innovations of far-reaching importance.

The sheer unpredictability of the harmony, the use of silence and the attention to sonority, (examples of which can be found in the first few pages) create a feeling of improvisation and the listener is obliged to experience the work totally in the present. These qualities are a reflection of Debussy's openness to influences outside the Western tradition, such as the colorful work of the emerging Russian nationalists and the Oriental music first encountered at the 1889 Paris Exposition. Of equal importance was the dark writing of Poe (1809–49), and the symbolist poetry of Baudelaire (1821–67) and Mallarmé (1842–1898).

Debussy's art is one of suggestion and these exotic sources offered some intriguing possibilities to him, the most celebrated of them being the unusual scales such as the pentatonic and whole tone. Together with the old church modes, so beloved by French composers, this amounted to a veritable treasure chest of melodic and harmonic novelty and it reinforced Debussy's consideration of harmony as color rather than function. A fine instance is the piano prelude **Voiles**, from the First Book, a ternary structure whose outer sections are written entirely in the whole tone scale, the short central section in the pentatonic corresponding to the black keys of the piano.

Debussy made further excursions into new harmonic territory, experimenting with non-triadic structures, for example, chords of superimposed fourths and fifths (the opening of **La cathédrale engloutie**) and finding particularly the dominant seventh open to all sorts of possibilities, from chromatic alteration to the addition of ninths, elevenths and thirteenths. More importantly, chords could be connected by intuition rather than by the "laws" of harmony. They could also stand alone with no need of resolution. The mysterious quality this gave was enhanced by the position of the chords in musical space and the instrumental color allotted to them (the evanescent nature of the piano's sound was wonderfully exploited in this respect). As a result, Debussy's music has a fluid and slightly restless quality, perfect for the suggestibility he desired.

FREE ATONALITY

But for all the breadth of Satie's and Debussy's innovations, there was no feeling of any crisis of tonality such as was being experienced in Vienna. Exotic elements, color harmony, looser structure, modality (even the ambiguous variety used by Satie) and so on were brought in to renew the language, not take it to the edge of extinction. In Vienna, as we have seen, the edge had been reached and some, like Mahler, had already peered over. (The terrifying chord, made up of ten different notes, which appears at the climax of the one completed movement of his **Tenth Symphony** (1909–10), shown in Example 2, is surely an expression of this.)

Ex.2 Mahler, Symphony No.10. 1st movement, bar 206

What was a nightmare for Mahler was, however, a challenge for Arnold Schoenberg (1874–1951) and his two most important pupils Anton Webern (1883–1945) and Alban Berg (1885–1935). The age gap between master and pupils of this so-called Second Viennese School can safely be ignored for the careers of all three followed remarkably similar and parallel lines. The ultra-expressive, intensely chromatic world of late Romanticism was their heritage and their early works show considerable confidence in not only handling the style, but also stretching its possibilities to the limits.

There was, however, with the notable exception of Schoenberg's gargantuan **Gurrelieder** (1900–10), an instinctive shying away from expansiveness and a greater concern for tightness of structure, as if mindful of the destructive power of advanced chromaticism. Wagner's leitmotiv technique was a useful model and a supreme vindication of it can be found in Berg's **Piano Sonata** (1907–8) which is held together entirely by a rigorous deployment of thematic motifs and not at all by the advertised key of B minor.

Contemporary with this work is Schoenberg's **Second String Quartet**. The internal organization here owes more to Brahms and what Schoenberg identified as Brahms' technique of "developing variation" but the grip of the keys chosen for the first three movements is just as precarious as in Berg's Sonata, if not more so.

The novel decision to include settings for soprano of two poems by the German expressionist poet Stefan George (1868–1933), as the final two movements of the Quartet was of considerable, perhaps symbolic, significance. The first line of the poem chosen for the final movement, *Entrückung*, translates as "I feel air from another planet" and Schoenberg's response was to take the suspension of tonality a step further, creating a kind of harmonic no-man's land where chords with vague tonal references (including actual triads) co-exist with others of an entirely ambiguous nature, all made to work by the composer's careful voice-leading and motivic technique. The movement does end, uneasily, in F# major, connecting with the distant memory of the work's opening in F# minor, but the breakthrough had been made.

In his next work, the **Three Piano Pieces Op.11** of 1909, Schoenberg finally dispenses with tonality altogether, and with it the distinction between dissonance and consonance. It is important to stress, however, that Schoenberg was not interested in effecting a complete break with the past. His abandoning of tonality was not accompanied by an abandoning of compositional techniques. The first piece in the Op.11 set makes this clear at the outset. There is continual development and variation of motifs and Schoenberg even succeeds in creating a kind of harmonic movement through voice-leading.

In the second piece, Schoenberg, as if to reinforce his intentions, spins his material over a pedal point; one which, moreover, incorporates an oscillating minor third, D – F, in an unmistakable reference to Mahler and the key of D minor. Clearly, the process was painful – certainly tentative – and one could argue that at times the *sound* of these two pieces is not so far removed from that of Mahler, though the third is more unremittingly dissonant. The important thing for Schoenberg, however, was that from now on any type of chord-structure was permissible. The imagination could take over.

Problems of Form

Thus began a period of almost fifteen years of unprecedented freedom for the three Viennese composers. There was a price, however. The loss of the organizing power of tonality became a real handicap when it came to large-scale composition, unless there was a text or program on which to hang the music. (Berg's first opera, **Wozzeck**, completed in 1922, is a superb example of what can be achieved when a fertile and febrile imagination is put to work on a story of mental breakdown and murder.)

Not surprisingly, therefore, Schoenberg, Berg and Webern began the cultivation of small-scale pieces, typically about three to six per set and titled purely functionally. Characteristic examples are Schoenberg's **Six Little Piano Pieces Op.19** (1911), Berg's **Four Pieces for Clarinet and Piano Op.5** (1913) and Webern's **Five Movements for String Quartet Op.5** (1909). Some of the individual pieces in these sets, the last of Schoenberg's Op.19 for instance, are only a few measures long, lasting just a few seconds.

More ambitious is Berg's **Three Pieces for Orchestra Op.6** (1915) a work showing a remarkably sure handling of free atonality over the twenty minutes or so of its duration (the individual pieces last, respectively, five, five and ten minutes). But whatever the length of these works, they are never short on emotional content. Webern, in particular, packs an enormous amount of detail into the short time-frames of his works, investing almost every note or tiny phrase with a separate dynamic profile, articulation and color. The concentrated, aphoristic miniature became, in fact, the preferred vehicle for Webern's ideas, even when dealing with sonata form, whose span is always characteristically reduced.

EMANCIPATION CONTINUES

If Schoenberg felt responsible for emancipating dissonance, there were many other composers walking the fine line between expanded tonality and free atonality. One of the most familiar names is that of Alexander Scriabin (1872–1915). Motivated by an intense, mystical desire to unite all the arts and the senses, he developed a highly evocative brand of chromaticism which exploits the ambiguities of chromatically altered chords, playing on their effect in an almost Debussyan manner.

The combined influence of Scriabin and Debussy is evident in the sensuous and perfumed harmonic world of the Polish composer Karol Szymanowski (1882–1937). By contrast, the fantastic flights of imagination in the early work of Sergei Prokofiev (1891–1953), such as the aptly-named **Sarcasmes** (1912) for piano or the **Second Piano Concerto** (1913, rewritten 1923), give rise to chromaticism of a more acerbic, pungent type, helped along by a rhythmic vitality comparable to Stravinsky's.

There is no doubt that the new idiom, with its absence of any kind of restraint, was ideally suitable for the involvement the three Viennese, and some of their contemporaries, had with the current wave of Expressionism. To this end they explored new and unusual instrumental and vocal timbres such as *col legno, sul ponticello* and harmonics for the strings, mutes for strings and brass and Sprechgesang (a type of vocal performance between singing and speaking, notated by using crosses for note-heads), which found its most effective employment in Schoenberg's **Pierrot Lunaire** (1921). They gave greater emphasis also to dynamics; sudden, violent changes being quite common. Most crucially, they developed a way of continually rotating the twelve semitones so as to prevent the music from sounding even vaguely tonal.

NEW ASPECTS OF TIMBRE

There is, in fact, much in common between the works of French, Viennese, Russian and other composers at this period in and around the First World War, particularly in terms of the sensation of harmony and sound in general. In Schoenberg's Op.19 pieces, mentioned above, the veiled tonality of No.2 and the tolling-bell effects of No.6 are not so far removed from some of Debussy's intimate soundscapes. Webern's scrupulous attention to all aspects of sonority is also very close to the ideals of the French master, despite the differences in intent.

In Debussy's **Nuages** (Clouds), the first of the three orchestral **Nocturnes**, written as long ago as 1899, the opening organum-like progression of intervals on two clarinets doubled at the lower octave by two bassoons is momentarily colored, in the third measure, by an oboe shadowing the first clarinet, as though the clouds have undergone a touch of grey for a few seconds. The oboe is surely not meant to be heard but rather felt as a modification of the clarinet's timbre.

A similar type of sensitivity to timbre occurs at the end of the first of Webern's **Five Pieces for Orchestra Op.10** (1913) where four F naturals are each given a separate tone-color, viz. note 1, muted trumpet; note 2, flute and muted trumpet; note 3, flute; note 4, celeste. This is a very subtle example of what is called Klangfarbenmelodie (lit. melody of sound-colors) but it can also be regarded as a modulation of timbre; muted trumpet to flute via a combination of both, with the celeste as a kind of final echo.

Rhythm

Innovations in rhythm to match those in harmony and timbre are not normally associated with the Viennese and French composers of this period, but the avoidance of regular pulsation is certainly noticeable in their music, except when dance idioms are being employed. In general, Debussy's expressive aims demanded a greater fluidity and irregularity of rhythm, which also suited the expressionism of the Viennese. Webern, especially, would have instinctively felt that the tiny gestures which constituted the material of his evolving style worked best in a metrically free environment. He was also one of the first composers to use constantly changing time-signatures, thus enhancing the metrical freedom. (In a characteristic act of perversity, Satie preferred to omit bar-lines altogether, even if the music was metrically regular.)

The freeing of rhythm as a by-product of expression is one thing, the exploitation of rhythm for its own sake is entirely another. Perhaps not surprisingly, the impetus for this came from outside the symphonic tradition. The Russian nationalists had for some time been carving out an alternative route with their colorful orchestration and folk music-inspired melodies and modal harmonies.

When Igor Stravinsky (1882–1971) made his first entry onto the world stage in 1910 with his ballet **The Firebird**, written for Diaghilev's Ballets Russes, he appeared to be continuing the tradition, following in the footsteps of his teacher Rimsky-Korsakov (1844–1908). But within three years, Stravinsky had written two more ballet scores for Diaghilev, **Petrouchka** (1911) and **The Rite of Spring** (1913), whose stories, rooted in Russian folklore, had unlocked in the composer a musical revolution the like of which had never before been experienced and which still reverberates to this day.

If **The Rite of Spring** has taken the credit for its rhythmic innovations which have changed music forever, this should not blind us to what Stravinsky achieved in **Petrouchka**, which is far closer in this respect to **The Rite** than it is to **The Firebird**. The inventiveness in orchestration, harmony and rhythm is truly astonishing. It was in **Petrouchka** that Stravinsky began to develop the fractured rhythms, explosive interruptions, irregular accents and above all the strikingly scored, tonally ambiguous and primitive-sounding ostinati that resurface with such violence in **The Rite**. (Tonally ambiguous ostinati were to become a feature of Satie's work, as we have noted above.)

The real breakthrough, however, is the way in which pitch-content and instrumental timbre are made subservient to the rhythm, throwing it into greater relief. In the dance of the peasant with his bear from **Petrouchka**, both the pitches and the sonority serve to "color" the heavy, plodding ostinato which accompanies the shrieking melody, played by two clarinets in unison. Melody is still a strong presence in this ballet and the ostinati remain as accompaniments, whatever their novelty.

The repeated bitonal chord (see Example 3) at the opening of the *Augurs of Spring* section of **The Rite** acts, like the **Petrouchka** example, as a substitute for stamping feet, or perhaps a drum, the two components of the chord, an Fb major triad and an Eb7, cancelling each other out to produce a neutral sonority, reinforced by the undifferentiated color of strings-plus-horns.

Ex.3   Stravinsky, The Rite of Spring ('Augurs of Spring'); bitonal chord

© Copyright 1912, 1921 by Hawkes & Son (London) Ltd. Used by permission of Boosey & Hawkes Music Publishers Ltd.

More significant, though, is the way this entire section is dominated by the eighth-note pulse, set up so strongly at the beginning. Notwithstanding the melodic fragments which are incorporated in the texture, as well as the various ostinato figures, it is the rhythm which propels the music and becomes the focus of attention.

It is, however, **The Rite**'s final section, the *Sacrificial Dance*, which contains Stravinsky's greatest innovations in rhythm. Responding to the frenzy of the girl dancing herself to death, he found himself inventing a completely new technique whereby small rhythmic cells are varied by irregular repetition and juxtaposition. Accents fall unpredictably and the time signature changes constantly. Almost nothing remains in the way of melody and harmony again has only a coloring function. In the *Sacrificial Dance*, Stravinsky finally manages to emancipate rhythm, developing it independently and allowing it to drive the music to its destination.

Stravinsky's Later Russian Works

Stravinsky's achievements in **Petrouchka** and **The Rite of Spring** cast a huge shadow over the compositions which followed during the remaining years of the decade – Stravinsky's so-called "Russian" period. Most of these pieces have Russian themes, though Stravinsky preferred French titles: **Renard** (1915–16), a Burlesque on Russian folk tales; the two small song-cycles **Pribaoutki** (1914) and **Berceuses du chat** (1915–16); **L'histoire du soldat** (1918), a theatrical piece 'to be read, played and danced' and **Les noces**, described as a 'Russian choreographic scene', written between 1914 and 1917 though not reaching its definitive version until 1923.

Among the purely instrumental works of this period, the **Three Pieces for String Quartet** (1914) is a unique contribution to the genre. In the first piece, all four instruments are given completely separate roles and separate groups of pitches, but all combine in an evocation of a peasant dance complete with hurdy-gurdy drone.

In all these works, Stravinsky was inspired by Russian folk melodies while continuing to develop the harmonic and rhythmic preoccupations of the earlier ballets. In addition, there is the ongoing refinement of his extraordinary ear for sonority. The works cited above all feature instrumental forces which are not only unconventional but also unique to the work in question. The **Berceuses du chat**, for example, uses just three clarinets whereas **Les noces**, whose scoring gave the composer so much trouble, calls for an ensemble of four pianos and percussion.

The instrumentation of **L'histoire du soldat** (violin, double bass, clarinet, bassoon, cornet, trombone and percussion), reflects Stravinsky's interest, shared by many other composers, in jazz and ragtime, musical idioms which offered more possibilities to his always inquisitive mind.

This attitude towards instrumentation was often governed by economic necessity (touring small numbers of performers was an unavoidable consequence of the war years), but it was also a reaction against the symphony orchestra as an institution which many saw as an outmoded symbol of nineteenth century Romanticism. The trend has continued to the present day and the programming of works like Stravinsky's **Ragtime** (1918), which is scored for flute, clarinet, horn, trumpet, trombone, violin, viola, double bass, percussion and cimbalom, and lasts a little over four minutes, still presents a problem to conductors and promoters.

SEEDS OF CHANGE

The climax of this period in Stravinsky's career was the composition of the **Symphonies of Wind Instruments** (1920). The importance of this work lies in the way different combinations of instruments are given different sorts of material of varying lengths, which are simply juxtaposed without any kind of linking. These blocks of material (about thirteen separate ones can be distinguished), are rotated in an unpredictable fashion, seemingly according to Stravinsky's intuition, but on each reappearance they are subjected to subtle variation: contraction, expansion, transposition, slight changes in instrumentation or internal rhythmic organization are the most common. The method has its origin, of course, in **The Rite**, but here there is no external program, just the sound of the instruments. The work's detached quality can be seen as a reaction against expressiveness and/or as anticipating the composer's neo-classical phase which was to follow, but Stravinsky's dedication of the piece to Debussy's memory is a clear acknowledgement of the crucial role which the latter played in the emancipation of sound from context.

Varèse

The French-born Edgard Varèse (1883–1965) has always been perceived as being on the periphery of developments in modern music. The uncompromising nature of his music, with its emphasis on percussion and massive sound-complexes involving a high degree of dissonance, certainly reinforce the image of a man outside the mainstream, pursuing a totally independent path. There is, indeed, some truth in this as Varèse's views on music were rather unorthodox. Through his interest in science and the natural world, he came to regard sound from a scientific perspective: as essentially vibration with a complex inner structure.

Music he regarded as "organized sound". He expressed dissatisfaction with conventional musical instruments and their apparent limitations, calling for new ones to be developed, with the help of scientists and technicians. In this he was influenced by the views of his teacher Ferruccio Busoni (1866–1924) and also came close to the ideals of the Italian Futurists, Luigi Russolo (1885–1947), Filippo Marinetti (1876–1944) and others, who had called for an "Art of Noises" to celebrate the modern world of machines, airplanes and factories. But Varèse's ambitions were far loftier than the naive efforts of the Futurists.

Rather than simply present noises in simple combinations, he aimed to transform noise into music (for which he was later severely, if unfairly, criticized by the more "purist" John Cage).[2]

Powerful, raw, monumental: these are some of the words which come to mind when faced by Varèse's music. These qualities are seen to advantage in the handful of works written after his emigration to America in 1915, especially those for chamber ensembles and bearing scientific titles: **Hyperprism** (1922–23); **Intégrales** (1924), both scored for wind instruments and large percussion section; and the notorious **Ionisation** (1930–31) for 13 percussionists, the first major composition for percussion alone.

Two aspects of this music immediately strike the listener: the piling up of pitches to form vertical blocks of sound, and an almost violent use of dynamics, featuring sudden *sforzandi*, *crescendi* and, a favorite device, the accent at the *end* of a *crescendo*, the result of hearing recordings of sounds played backwards. In a real sense, the vertical sound-blocks and dynamic profiles are Varèse's substitutes for harmony and melody respectively. As might be expected, there is also considerable rhythmic freedom, due as much to the presence of the percussion as the composer's desire for a sound quality which is dynamic, fluid, unpredictable yet inexorable, like the course of a mighty river.

The opening of **Intégrales** shows Varèse's method clearly. The "melodic" interest is given to Eb clarinet, oboe and muted trumpet who take it in turns to perform variations on a high Bb: decorating it with other pitches, repeating it in different rhythms and applying varying dynamics. This line is not so much harmonized but sliced through by reiterations of a dissonant 6-note chord on clarinet, piccolos and trombones which is also subjected to rhythmic and dynamic variation. The percussion provides an independent, constantly changing carpet of rhythms and textures. This is the naked power of sound itself and its impact is almost physical.

There is also a strong underlying sense of frustration in Varèse's work. His dissatisfaction with conventional instruments, noted above, meant that he was always compromising between what he wanted to hear and what he could actually achieve. His frequent use of the siren indicates an imagination hearing things beyond the scope of the musical instruments of man. This may help to explain his small output but, ironically, when the means to realize his ideas became available around the time of the Second World War, with the invention of the tape recorder and the development of electronic music, Varèse only managed to complete a few passages of "organized electronic sound" to be inserted – optionally! – into the chamber piece **Déserts,** composed between 1945 and 1954 and the **Poème électronique** of 1958. Nevertheless, Varèse remains one of the true originals of twentieth century music, a real pioneer in his adopted country, which would soon witness the appearance of several more.

2
NATIONALISM, FOLK MUSIC, EXOTICISM

MUSICAL NATIONALISM, INCREASINGLY AN IMPORTANT part of the nineteenth century soundscape, gathered real momentum during the early years of the twentieth century as more composers began to plunder the rich treasures of their countries' folk heritages in order to find the bases from which to create new expressive languages, independent from the European mainstream.

BARTÓK

Mention has already been made of Stravinsky's use of Russian folk music. During the time of his greatest involvement with it, a more scientific approach had already begun a little further to the west, with the systematic collection, transcription and cataloguing of folk melodies from Hungary, Rumania and the Balkans by Béla Bartók (1881–1945), for whom they were to become an abundant source of rhythmic and melodic ideas. These tunes, with their often angular melodic intervals and speech-rhythms, were at first used unaltered and with a simple accompaniment. Gradually, through increased familiarity, they became assimilated and were absorbed into Bartók's own style. So complete was the process that it is sometimes difficult to say whether a given melody is a folk song or a Bartók invention. The tune which constitutes the theme of the finale of his **Fourth String Quartet** (1928), for example, is Bartók's own but it has all the qualities of the model (*see* Example 4).

The accompaniment, a repeated, syncopated dissonance, is not dissimilar to, and has the same function as, the chord used by Stravinsky in the Augurs of Spring section of **The Rite** (cf. Ex.3 above), by which it may also have been influenced. Both chords are neutral and percussive and, just as Stravinsky uses the pitch content of his chord to generate further material, so Bartók derives his chord from the pitches of the melody. (The chord may be viewed as either a pair of tritones a semitone apart, or as a perfect fifth with adjacent dissonant semitones.)

There is no doubt, too, that Bartók was influenced by the performance practice of the peasants whose songs and dances he collected. (The finale of the **Fourth String Quartet** is a virtual authentic peasant dance.) The harmonic idiom he developed, where minor seconds, sevenths and ninths and tritones predominate, gives exactly the right sort of piquancy to set off the melodies.

Ex.4   Bartók String Quartet No.4, fifth movement, opening

© Copyright 1929 by Universal Edition. © Copyright renewed 1956 by Boosey & Hawkes Inc. New York. Reproduced by permission. All rights reserved.

The tight organization shown in the interdependence of melodic and harmonic materials was typical of Bartók, for whom musical structure was a reflection of the forms and growth patterns of nature. Mirror forms and other symmetrical arrangements of pitches, both melodically and harmonically, are a common feature of Bartók's music. One such is the interval of a tritone (augmented fourth), whose position at the exact center of the octave means that it lends itself perfectly to all manner of symmetrical structures. The first movement of his great masterpiece, the **Music for String Instruments, Percussion and Celesta** (1936), opens with a fugal exposition whose subject is a sinuous, chromatic phrase, starting on middle A and generating a dense web of counterpoint before climaxing on multiple E flats; the distance of a tritone. The emphasis on E flat gives that note a kind of dominant function and the music gradually winds its way down to a solitary A via, at the end, a series of phrases from the fugue subject sounding against mirror images of themselves.

ENGLAND

After the death of Henry Purcell in 1695, England produced no major composers until the latter half of the nineteenth century when an unprecedentedly large number appeared, as well as several minor ones; altogether close to two dozen over a period of 60 years. In no way could the whole procession be called a school though one might, with some justification, call it a movement since there was a fairly widespread desire among them to revitalize and continue the country's great musical heritage, so long dormant.

The choral tradition, one of the glories of English music from the Elizabethan and Tudor periods through to the anglicized Handel, was an obvious attraction and a steady stream of works, particularly oratorios, was created, mostly pale imitations of Handel and Mendelssohn and most now largely forgotten, but including some outstanding achievements, such as Elgar's **The Dream of Gerontius** (1899–1900), very much in the English choral tradition, Holst's **The Hymn of Jesus** (1917) and Walton's **Belshazzar's Feast** (1930–1; rev.1948 & '59), both more forward-looking, especially with regard to harmony and rhythm.

The string consort music of England's golden age was another source and it was the idea of W.W. Cobbett (1847–1937), a businessman and private patron, to instigate a series of competitions offering prizes for the composition of Phantasies; single movement works in an arch-shaped structure, made up of sequences of contrasting yet thematically related sections. Part of Cobbett's plan was to bring the freer structures of consort music, like the Fancy, up to date, as it were, by combining it with the sonata principle, especially the cyclic form practiced by Liszt, Franck and others. It was an ingenious idea, resulting in the composition of several substantial works, not necessarily labelled as Phantasies, however.

Probably the best known, as well as one of the most successful, is the **Phantasy Quartet** for oboe and strings (1932) by a young Benjamin Britten (1913–76) but the architectural plan can be seen in other non-Phantasy pieces such as the **Second Piano Trio** (1929) by Britten's teacher, Frank Bridge (1879–1941).

A third element in this reawakening was, of course, folk song, and here there is an almost exact parallel to the work of Bartók in the person of Ralph Vaughan Williams (1872–1958). Much of his fieldwork was done at the same time as Bartók's and he likewise went through an extensive process of assimilation, arriving at a point where his own melodic style was completely permeated with both the letter and the spirit of English folk song.

The thematic material which opens Vaughan Williams' **Fifth Symphony** (1938–43; rev.1951) (Example 5) is strongly related to English minor mode folk songs like "The Captain's Apprentice" (Example 6) which appears in the **Norfolk Rhapsody No.1** (1905–6). Little melodic turns in the original song are recycled, as it were, in the Symphony, in a way comparable to Bartók's methods.

Ex.5 Vaughan Williams, Symphony No.5, first movement, opening theme

© Copyright Oxford University Press 1946. Reproduced by permission.

Ex.6 Vaughan Williams, 'The Captain's Apprentice' (Norfolk Rhapsody)

Oboe + violas

© Copyright Oxford University Press 1925. Reproduced by permission.

English folk songs, whether wistful or jolly, demand a completely different harmonic setting from that which Bartók provided for his Eastern European examples, and Vaughan Williams drew on the heritage of Tudor church music to evolve an idiom featuring major and minor triads, sometimes with added notes, in oblique and unconventional juxtapositions. The flavors thus obtained lend the music a strangely timeless and evocative, even visionary, quality, heard at its best in the celebrated **Fantasia on a Theme by Thomas Tallis** (1910; rev.1919).

Unfortunately, this idiom has given rise to the "pastoral" label often applied to Vaughan Williams and others of the English renaissance. This is a little unfair to Vaughan Williams, whose music is far more wide-ranging than the term suggests, though it has to be said that folk song is the single most important influence on his style. To some of these composers the label is not inappropriate – the work of George Butterworth (1885–1916) and Roger Quilter (1877–1953), for instance, is very much imbued with the spirit of English folk music though, again, European nineteenth century models, from Schumann to Fauré, are apparent in Quilter.

To others like Frank Bridge or Gustav Holst (1874–1934), who were much more aware of, and open to, the newer developments in European music, folk song offered one useful, though not indispensable or exclusive, source of inspiration. There are interesting cases, too, such as Arnold Bax (1883–1953) who, though born in London, developed a passion for things Celtic after extended stays on the west coasts of both Scotland and Ireland, resulting in a noticeable Celtic strain coloring his sumptuously late romantic idiom.

It is also worth noting that there were yet other composers in this movement who seemed to belong entirely to another world, like the francophile Lennox Berkeley (1903–89), whose style is much closer to that of his colleagues in France.

But the man who, to many people, has come to be regarded as the most representative of the English renaissance, Edward Elgar (1857–1934), remained apart from the folklorists yet his music, generously melodic, stately and positive, manages to convey something of the soul of the English nation, at least as it was perceived then, at the height of the Empire.

This quality, plainly recognizable though it is to, one suspects, a fair number of people, is at the same time difficult to pin down. The broad, *cantabile* sweep of Elgar's melodic style is the legacy of the English choral tradition whereas his penchant for suspended and unprepared sevenths, as well as chromatic sequences, is part of the common harmonic vocabulary of the nineteenth century. It is the peculiar blending of these ingredients which goes to make up the special character of Elgar's style but, as with many other composers, the process remains mysterious. The main theme which opens the **First Symphony** (1908), with its characteristic marking *nobilmente* and its strong flavor of pageantry, is the quintessential Elgar statement. On the other hand, the strange chromatic descending chords (including augmented triads) over a pedal point which form part of the development section in the first movement of the **Second Symphony** (1909–11) are no less typical but seem to belong to an altogether more private world.

JANÁČEK

In the case of Leos Janáček (1854–1928) it was not only the folk song of his native Moravia that inspired him but also the speech patterns of ordinary people. These were likewise transcribed and studied and formed an important ingredient in Janáček's melodic style, one of the most distinctive of the early twentieth century. It is terse and short-winded but full of latent drama, and thus eminently suited to opera, a genre in which Janáček excelled.

The harrowing psychological dramas of **Jenufa** (1903) and **Katya Kabanova** (1921), two of the composer's most compelling operas, owe much of their intensity to the tightness of Janáček's phrase-structure, where the short speech-like patterns are often subjected to repetition. The style is also effective in articulating the hidden programs that underlie many of his instrumental works, for example the **String Quartet No.2 (Intimate Letters)** (1928).

SPAIN

Although her indigenous music was already familiar to the outside world, Spain similarly experienced an emergence of national artistic consciousness within her boundaries through the work of, among others, Isaac Albéniz (1860–1909), Enrique Granados (1867–1916) and Manuel de Falla (1876–1946). Their work naturally focussed on the numerous traditional dances of Spain, with their distinctive rhythmic patterns, highly emotional melodic contours and, of course, the peculiar guitaristic tang of clashing semitones in the harmony. The influence of the great nineteenth century Romantics is also very noticeable, especially in the piano writing of Albéniz and Granados, which unfortunately distils the music's Spanish character somewhat, rendering it more generally European.

Falla, on the other hand, was more successful at forging a synthesis of the Spanish and symphonic traditions, creating an original style which found its finest expression in such characteristic works as the ballet **El amor brujo** (1925) and the **Concerto for Harpsichord and Five Instruments** (1926). It is also true, however, that Falla was greatly impressed by the evocations of Spain by Debussy, to the extent that he found himself, ironically, influenced by him. One is tempted to regard Falla's **Nights in the Gardens of Spain** (1916), a three-movement mini-piano concerto, as inspired as much by the second movement, **Iberia**, of Debussy's **Images** for orchestra (1906–12) as by the nocturnal atmosphere of Andalucia, Falla's own native province. The titles given by Falla to his three movements ('In the Generalife'; 'A Distant Dance'; 'In the Gardens of the Sierra de Córdoba') and his description of them as 'symphonic impressions' would appear to vindicate this view.

At any rate, Falla was not slow to recognize that Debussy's and, to a lesser extent, Ravel's Spanish impressions, were often superior to his own and those of his colleagues. It is undeniable that both Debussy and Ravel exhibited, through genuine sympathy, a thorough mastery of the Spanish idioms. Debussy only visited Spain in his mind, yet he showed an uncanny understanding of the country's musical essence.

Falla singled out in particular Debussy's **La soirée dans Grenade** (from the **Estampes** for piano, written in 1903) as being a "miraculous" evocation of the true spirit of Andalucia: "the truth without the authenticity".[3]

Ravel, on the other hand, was of partly Spanish descent, making his intimacy with Spanish music more natural, and there is a confidence in his handling of the style which places works like **Alborada del gracioso** (1905) above mere tone painting.

Debussy and Ravel were not only successful in their appropriation of Spanish music. Both composers, and several others, had witnessed at first hand the gamelan music of Indonesia at the Paris Exhibition of 1889, and been captivated by the sheer beauty of the sound as well as intrigued by the novel modality of the music. In the third movement, *Laideronnette, impératrice des pagodes,* of his suite **Ma mère l'oye** (1908–10; orch.1911), Ravel even attempted a reconstruction of the pyramid of melodies effect used in gamelan music.

Popular Culture

A further fascination, already mentioned in connection with Satie, was for the American popular music which had been infiltrating Parisian society since about the same time and was at the height of its popularity during and after the First World War. Paris was generally perceived as the cultural capital of Europe, and the composers based there, French or otherwise, were the first to experience this music. But it soon began to attract the attention of other composers further afield, such as William Walton (1902–83) in England, Paul Hindemith (1895–1963) in Germany and Dmitri Shostakovich (1906–75) in Russia.

Some varieties of the music were relatively easy to mimic. The syncopated rhythms and two-step beat of ragtime and its related forms, as much a novelty in those days as the gamelan, were quickly seized on by composers eager to breathe fresh life into this aspect of their craft. Debussy's ***Golliwog's Cake-Walk***, from the **Children's Corner Suite** (1906–8) is perhaps the best-known of many pieces which attempted to turn the idiom into art and it shares the same kind of dignified sedateness which is found in many of the piano rags of Scott Joplin (1868–1917), reminding us that this was indeed a serious art form; primarily a music to be listened to.

The transference of the idiom into the dance halls of the period introduced a more exuberant, extrovert edge and this is echoed in pieces like **La revue de cuisine** (The Kitchen Revue) (1927), a surrealist ballet by the Czech composer Bohuslav Martinů (1890–1959), the third movement of which is a Charleston, authentic not only rhythmically, but melodically and harmonically too, and capturing all the wild abandon of this most popular of dances.

Jazz proved a more problematical style and few composers were really successful at dealing with it. Despite his apparent enthusiasm, Stravinsky completely failed to understand its true nature, even when commissioned by the American bandleader Woody Herman (1913–87) to write the **Ebony Concerto** for his big band in 1945. Apart from a few 'wah wah' effects for muted trumpets, the work has nothing to do with jazz and it remains the one historical style he was unable to reinvent. Ravel, in his **Piano Concerto in G** (1931), came much closer, integrating the gestures of jazz with the same degree of skill he had shown with the music of Spain. Martinů, who, like Ravel, was genuinely interested in the music, also had some success in coming to grips with the idiom.

But it was undoubtedly Darius Milhaud (1892–1974) who was most able to appreciate the intricacies of instrumental texture, and even the "feel", in a typical jazz performance. His 1923 Negro ballet, **La création du monde**, features a marvellously accurate and faithful recreation of the spontaneity of group improvisation, but without actually asking the players to improvise. The masterly integration of jazz style and Milhaud's own brand of mainstream modernism within a tightly organized structure is neither patronizing nor mere pastiche but rather demonstrates that, in sympathetic hands, apparently conflicting idioms can be compatible. It makes for compelling listening.

The composers mentioned above were all, of course, looking at jazz and popular music from the 'classical' perspective. In the case of George Gershwin (1898–1937) we have an example of someone attacking the problem, as it were, from the other side of the fence. As a gifted writer of jazz-tinged popular songs, Gershwin had an advantage over his classical colleagues. The problem, for him, lay in the art of symphonic development of ideas. From this viewpoint, his **Rhapsody in Blue** (1924), with its necessarily freer structure, is more successful than his **Piano Concerto in F** (1925), where the need for tighter organization is not so satisfactorily met. His opera **Porgy and Bess** (1935), however, sees Gershwin responding to the highly dramatic plot with music (not just songs!) of great power and emotional depth.

THE EXOTIC

We have entered here into an aspect of early twentieth century music destined to be of great consequence. The discovery and use of "exotic" musical cultures is the other side of the nationalist coin. Composers who are drawn to exoticism are not nationalists in the same sense as are Bartók or Vaughan Williams, since their own folk music is not central to their styles. They are rather early examples of what we might call cultural tourists, and their work foreshadows later similar manifestations of eclecticism like polystylism and the various types of crossover. Both nationalism and exoticism can be regarded as part of the search for new means of expression.

And as new pockets of nationalism have continued to emerge onto the world stage during the century – in South America, Asia, Northern Europe and Africa – so attempts at cross-fertilization have continued to be made.

SOUTH AMERICA

In the case of South America, the profile of her indigenous composers has been unfortunately overshadowed by the universal popularity of the region's various dances and their appropriation by 'foreign' composers. Darius Milhaud was among the first to discover and make use of this music when he accompanied the poet Paul Claudel, just appointed Minister to Brazil, on a trip to that country in 1917. But, with the possible exception of the Brazilian Heitor Villa-Lobos (1887–1959), whose fame rests largely on a novel blending of Brazilian folk rhythms and Bachian counterpoint in his series of nine suites for various forces entitled **Bachianas brasileiras** (1930–45), South American composers remain unknown to the majority of the public.

Villa-Lobos himself produced a huge quantity of music in all genres, but it is seldom played and his contemporaries have hardly fared any better. This neglect is regrettable since even a modest investigation reveals some quite outstanding and original music by such talented figures as the Mexicans Silvestre Revueltas (1899–1940) and Carlos Chávez (1899–1978) and the Argentinian Alberto Ginastera (1916–83).

One composer who has achieved something of a cult status is Astor Piazzolla (1921–92), also from Argentina, who tried to elevate the country's national dance, the tango, to a higher artistic level. Unlike other 'folklorists', however, Piazzolla did not try to integrate the tango with the modernist mainstream, but rather borrowed freely from it, and also from jazz, while keeping the essential character of the dance intact.

Thus, although the form may be extended, fugal passages and improvisation introduced and some fairly simple but effective extended techniques employed, Piazzolla tended to remain faithful to the rhythm and moods of the tango proper. Furthermore, with a few exceptions, he preferred to work with his favored small ensemble of bandoneon (played by himself), piano, electric guitar, violin and double bass, which ensured a particular continuity and image and anchored the music more to the night club dance floor than the concert hall. In this way, Piazzolla distanced himself from the work of Bartók, Vaughan Williams and others and he remains a curious, isolated figure.

The Spirit of Independence – Ives and Cowell

The complexity and bewildering variety of which we spoke at the beginning of this section was a fact of life before a quarter of the century had passed. As composers from the United States rose to prominence during this period, the complexity was magnified. What was so crucial about the American input was that it showed that it was possible to create music of significance without the support of a long and weighty tradition, taking inspiration solely from the simple, ready-made musical forms of ordinary people; folk songs, dances, hymns and the like. To be sure, there were composers who chose to "buy into" the European tradition, as it were, by studying there. The great French teacher and champion of Stravinsky, Nadia Boulanger (1887–1979), was a magnet for many of them.

But in some ways a more typical composer was the one thrown back onto his own resources; who regarded Europe as too far away to be relevant; and who put his trust in the truth of immediate experience – in short, a pioneer. Several such figures were to appear during the century: one-off, independent, maverick types; 'desert plants' in Walter Zimmermann's happy coinage[4]. Their *cartes blanches* were given by the man who has come to epitomize the pioneering spirit in music – Charles Ives (1874–1954).

However much Ives knew of the work of his European contemporaries, and he knew much more than is often believed, he certainly kept it at arm's length, preferring to solve his compositional problems individually and according to his own experience and intuition. In this he was following the example set by his father George, who had a profound effect on his son's musical development. Ives senior stressed the importance of direct experience, of experimentation and open-mindedness rather than slavery to habit and of the responsibility of the artist first and foremost to himself. Added to this was his fascination with sound and the way it behaved in different circumstances.

Thus the grandiose thoughts expressed in the song **from 'Paracelsus'** (a 1921 setting of Browning) elicit from Ives a piano part of great complexity, the harmony moving between simple tonal structures, bitonality and atonality as the words dictate. The song is metrically free, at one point the piano given a series of bitonal chords in semibreves, presumably to be played evenly but freely and independently of the vocal part, though no such indication is given. Thus also the phenomenon of several bands all playing different tunes simultaneously on public holidays, which Ives heard as a young boy, is recycled in his tone-poem **The Fourth of July** (1908), the orchestra divided up into independent groupings to reproduce the same effect.

Sometimes the search for truth would lead to highly unorthodox solutions like the one which occurs at the end of the last movement of the **Piano Sonata No.2 (Concord, Mass.,1840–1860),** written between 1910 and 1915. This movement is a portrait of Henry David Thoreau (1817–62), one of a group of transcendentalist writers whose thinking was a great influence on the composer, and Ives asks that the melodic line which depicts Thoreau's own flute playing by the shore of Walden Pond should be played by an actual flute.

With Ives, the musical idea was always more important than questions of what was practical. This intractable quality got him into deep water with performers, even the most willing, but his insatiable quest for truth of expression was an important lesson for future generations of American composers who could now express their relationship with the world as they saw it, and with their own language if necessary.

An immediate beneficiary of Ives's legacy was Henry Cowell (1897–1965), who befriended the older man and was a tireless champion of his music. Of a similarly experimental turn of mind, though in some ways more practical, Cowell produced a large and incredibly varied amount of music before he was barely into his thirties and which covered an even greater range of innovation than that of Ives. He went further into areas of rhythmic and metric complexity, largely as a result of his researches into the nature of sound and vibration (anticipating Stockhausen's work in the 1950s), as well as ultra-chromaticism.

An Ivesian fearless naivety must have gone into Cowell's discovery of new sounds that could be produced on the piano. One of these was the tone cluster; a largish group of simultaneously sounded adjacent notes, articulated by the flat of the hand, the fist or the forearm as necessary. This effect, which caught the attention of Bartók, appears in many of the startlingly original short piano pieces of the 1910s and 1920s.

Perhaps even more daring was Cowell's exploration of the possibilities of playing directly on the piano's strings, by plucking them, sweeping across and along them with the hand or striking them with some implement or other. These techniques can be heard spectacularly in **The Banshee** (1925), a totally unprecedented and astonishingly early piece of experimentation, whose sound-world eerily anticipates electro-acoustic music.

Later on, Cowell's indefatigable curiosity led him to explore exotic musical cultures from all over the world, echoing the achievements of Debussy and others in Europe, but again going much further, seeking, as he put it, "to draw on those materials common to the music of all the peoples of the world [in order] to build a new music particularly related to our own century."[5] In this, Cowell became a key part of the continuing trend towards polystylism and ethnic crossover.

3
SERIALISM

SCHOENBERG, BERG AND WEBERN

THE OPEN SEA OF FREE atonality was really far too boundless for prolonged navigation. By the 1920s Schoenberg, at any rate, clearly began to feel the need for more control over his materials. Constitutionally closer to the Austro-German symphonic tradition than his pupils, he had never completely forsaken the ideal of a composition where everything was derived from one basic idea. (In an article on his teacher, written in 1912, Webern had marvelled at the fact that in the **First String Quartet, Op.7** (1905), "there is…not a single note…that does not have a thematic basis.")[6] In pursuit of this ideal, Schoenberg sought to integrate the organizational power of symphonic technique within the atonal universe he had been exploring since 1908.

His solution was to fix the order of the twelve semitones rather than have them constantly rotating according to his intuition. This ordering, the tone-row, or series, would remain fixed for the entire composition and be the source of all harmonic and melodic material. Permutations of the series could be obtained by first inverting it, then reversing both original and inverted forms. These four basic forms could be transposed onto any degree of the chromatic scale, giving forty eight possible variations of the same row of pitches. Schoenberg first tried out the new method in the third of the **Five Pieces for Piano, Op.23** (1923), but the first fully serial work was the **Suite for Piano, Op.25** of 1924.

Both Berg and Webern were drawn to the new method and it is instructive to compare the attitudes of all three composers to the principle of "composition with twelve tones related only to one another" as Schoenberg described it. Berg turned out to be the least committed, regarding serialism as just one of several possible methods which might even co-exist in the same piece.

His late masterpiece, the **Violin Concerto** (1935), is the most celebrated example of this inclusivity. The series, a succession of overlapping major and minor triads plus a fragment of a whole tone scale (Example 7) is deliberately fashioned to allow tonal references, including the famous quotation of the Lutheran chorale *Es ist genug,* in Bach's harmonization, and to guide the work towards its ending on a Bb6 chord (notes 1,2,3 and 12 of the original row).

Ex.7   Berg, Violin Concerto (note row)

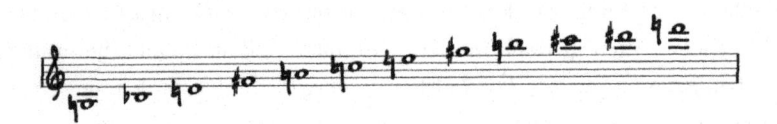

His second opera, **Lulu,** left unfinished at his death, is notable for the way Berg mixes serialism, tonality and free atonality together according to the demands of the drama. Berg was also adventurous in the way he derived new forms of the row by simple permutation or re-ordering, for example, taking alternate notes of the original and obtaining the sequence 1,4,7,10,2,5,8,11,3,6,9,12. Another method was to have two transpositions of the row stated simultaneously, the notes of one alternating with those of the other.

All this was utterly foreign to Schoenberg, who remained conservative in his use of the row, but Berg was perhaps demonstrating an inherent and fundamental weakness within the method which was that, in a typical row (i.e. one with no special characteristics), the harmonies produced tend to have a similar density and degree of dissonance, making any sense of harmonic progression impossible.

The problem can be observed in Schoenberg's **Fourth String Quartet** (1937) where the row, a relatively straightforward atonal set,[7] is completely incompatible with the spirit and style of the writing, which is largely derived from the nineteenth century symphonic tradition, with Brahms the obvious model. The continuous rotation of the various forms of the row is better suited to structures such as Variation form and, from this point of view, Schoenberg's **Variations for Orchestra** (1926–8) is infinitely more satisfying.

The greater flexibility shown by Berg, both in the type and treatment of the row, would appear to have been a shrewd judgment. The most outwardly Romantic of the three Viennese, he needed the broader canvas for his wide-ranging, expressionist art. Webern, on the other hand, saw in serial technique the means to achieve the concentrated clarity of form and content he wanted.

Where Berg sought to increase the row's possibilities, Webern sought to reduce them. The Webernian row often has a limited number of basic forms. That of the **Symphony, Op.21** (1928) is an intervallic palindrome, there being, consequently, no independent retrograde form. That of the **String Quartet, Op.28** (1938) is three permutations of the B A C H motif (the German spelling of Bb,A,C,B), itself limited to only two intervals – semitone and minor third. The *ne plus ultra*, however, is the **Concerto for Nine Instruments, Op.24** (1934), whose row is made up of four permutations of a three-note cell, the last three being, respectively, the retrograde-inversion, inversion and retrograde of the first, suitably transposed so as to produce a 12 note series; Schoenberg's serial universe in miniature (see Example 8).

Ex.8 Webern, Concerto Op.24 (note row)

© Copyright 1948 by Universal Edition, A.G. Wien. Reproduced by permission. All rights reserved.

The restrictions thus imposed on melody and harmony are clearly severe. It is equally clear that Webern is not concerned with such matters; at least not as usually understood. Instead of melody and harmony – the horizontal and vertical axes of conventional music – Webern gives us a sound-field populated solely by the motif: presented linearly as a phrase, simultaneously as a chord, fragmented further or juxtaposed with other forms of itself. By restricting the palette in this way, the listener's attention is drawn more towards the motif and the different forms it is made to assume, as well as its intervallic structure, its register, timbre, rhythmic profile and dynamic level. Webern's elevation of these parameters to a level of prime importance is one of the most significant aspects of his work, one which was to have tremendous consequences for the next generation of serial composers.

THE EARLY WORK OF JOHN CAGE

Schoenberg was one among several European Jewish composers who moved to America to escape the Nazis, settling in California in 1933. His reputation as the instigator of serialism made him a magnet for young American composers, though he was adamant about not teaching the method, regarding it as chiefly a personal solution to his own compositional problems.

This did not prevent the method from attracting new adherents, of course. Milton Babbitt (b.1916) is probably the best-known of this generation, though his work only began in earnest during the later 1940s. But Schoenberg had an immediate and decisive effect on a young, inexperienced composer by the name of John Cage (1912–92). (Cage's meeting with Schoenberg, his reverence for him and his accounts of the classes he attended have been well documented, by Cage and others.)[8]

Cage was already using a type of proto-serialism at the time he met Schoenberg and continued to develop a personal methodology, working with small motifs taken from the rows. Later, however, Cage began gravitating towards writing for percussion, largely as a result of his work with modern dance groups, and here the experience with serialism proved useful. Matching percussion music to choreography necessitated an organization of rhythm and Cage developed a technique whereby beats are grouped together according to a sequence of numbers.

A later refinement of this technique involved having a number sequence govern everything from the number of measures per phrase to the number of phrases per section and the number of sections in the piece. Cage referred to this as a micro-macrocosmic rhythmic structure and a particularly fine example is found in his percussion sextet **First Construction (In Metal)** of 1939, which employs the palindromic sequence 4,3,2,3,4.

The real novelty of Cage's music of this period, however, is its sound-world. Taking his cue from Cowell, and in the true spirit of the pioneer, Cage began a ruthless search for more instruments and other sound-sources to add to his already rapidly expanding arsenal of percussion. His search led to two major innovations. Firstly, the establishment of recording studios at this time made available electronic equipment – sound generators, filters, amplifiers, microphones, gramophones, etc. – whose creative potential Cage immediately saw, neatly bypassing its original purpose.

Thus was born the **Imaginary Landscape** series, the first of which, dating from 1939, uses gramophone recordings of test signals on which the performers play the notated rhythms by raising and lowering their styli. The speed of the turntables is altered by a clutch. The eerie, siren-like whines are accompanied by a Chinese cymbal and two Cowellian piano sounds: a sweeping of the bass strings with a soft beater, and a varied repetition of three notes played on the keyboard but muted by placing the fingers on the strings.

The second innovation came in 1940 with the invention of the prepared piano where small objects, such as screws, bolts, bits of rubber, etc. are fixed between the strings of a grand piano causing radical changes to the pitch, timbre and duration of the sounds and turning the instrument into a one-man percussion group. Cage's music for the prepared piano includes various chamber works as well as solo pieces, of which the best known is probably the **Sonatas and Interludes** (1946–48).

The works for prepared piano may be regarded as an extreme development of Cage's serial thinking, in that a given collection of preparations gives a fixed set of sonorities which are the only sounds in the piece and thus constitute a kind of "series". Cage had, in fact, experimented with using such fixed sets of sounds in a few instrumental works of this period, such as the **String Quartet in Four Parts** (1949–50).

Some of the prepared piano works only employ a few pitches anyway, making the serial connection more obvious. The **Sonatas and Interludes**, with its large number of prepared notes as well as some unprepared ones, is perhaps less clearly related. Cage was never particularly consistent.

Working with percussion and unconventional sound was pushing Cage more and more away from "accepted" musical sound and towards the world of noise, the divide at which, Cage thought, Varèse had failed. The role of silence was assuming greater significance for him too (he had noted that both sound and silence had duration in common and could therefore be incorporated equally in the rhythmic schemes he was devising.)

At the same time, Cage began his involvement with Eastern philosophy, at first that of India, later Zen Buddhism. Cage found here ample corroboration of where his work seemed to be heading but, more than that, they helped to initiate the next phase in Cage's development, probably the most controversial event in the history of music. This was his entry into the world of chance and, with this, Cage was about to change the face of music. We shall return to this later.

4
Neo-Classicism

THE CASTING OFF OF WHAT is 'sensuous' and the renunciation of subjectivity."[9] Ferruccio Busoni's words to the writer Paul Bekker describe his own position at the time (1920) with regard to composition but also stand as a motto for the other main strand of European modernism which began to gather momentum during the 1920s.

This was what came to be called Neo-classicism and its renunciation of subjectivity was a renunciation not only of Romanticism, but also Expressionism, Impressionism and Nationalism; all lumped together because of their shared adherence to the concept of music as an expressive medium. Busoni was really advocating a return to the ideal of pure, abstract music; music which existed simply for its own sake, even if, as may be argued, such music is a myth. Busoni was calling for a re-instatement of clean lines and uncluttered textures; melody, harmony and polyphony in perfect balance. Bach and Mozart were to be the models.

Ravel

After the cataclysm of the First World War, Europe was certainly receptive to such a change of direction and in Germany a new slogan was coined to describe it: Neue Sachlichkeit (new objectivity). As far as France was concerned, though, it was more a case of reinforcing an inherent characteristic.[10] The music of Ravel provides us with a clear example of how innovation can come from within an established tradition.

Though often linked with Debussy, whom he greatly admired, Ravel was spiritually closer to the formal perfection and clarity of the eighteenth century: Mozart and the French *clavecinistes*. Perfection of form was much more important to him than the floating, improvisatory approach of Debussy, and he thought of the art of composition as analogous to the production of a perfectly executed artefact.

The influence of the French eighteenth century is shown in Ravel's preference for old dance forms. The waltz is celebrated in the **Valses nobles et sentimentales** (1911, orch.1912), the middle movement of the **Sonatine for Piano** (1905) is a minuet and the suite **Le tombeau de Couperin** (1917, orch. 1919) contains a minuet, rigaudon and forlane.

What Debussy and Ravel did share was an enthusiasm for exotic musical cultures and for making new harmonic discoveries. In this latter capacity, Ravel went considerably further than his colleague in stretching the possibilities of chromatic alteration but, following the example of his teacher Fauré, he liked the added color of modal inflections and generally stuck to the principles of functional harmony, distancing himself further from Debussy's tendency to treat chords as ends in themselves.

Furthermore, the sensuous quality of Debussy's music is something that Ravel tried to avoid, or at least treated objectively though, if he were dealing with sensuousness, as in the **Trois poèmes de Stéphane Mallarmé** (1913), his harmony responded accordingly and these three settings, for voice, accompanied by two flutes, two clarinets, piano and string quartet, contain some of the most voluptuous, and advanced, harmony in his output.

By this time, Ravel had been exposed to the work of Schoenberg and the Mallarmé settings were greatly influenced, certainly in instrumentation, by his having heard **Pierrot lunaire**. Schoenberg's influence is also felt in Ravel's later song cycle, the **Chansons madécasses** (1925–6). The accompaniment here, of flute, cello and piano, is notable for its extremely dissonant harmony, with extensive uses of bitonality sometimes bordering on the atonal, and its contrapuntal texture, an unusual departure for Ravel. The second song, *Aoua!*, deals with the corrupting influence of the white man in an innocent tropical paradise and sees Ravel responding with sounds of unprecedented violence, for once stepping outside his normal cool, classical exterior as he gives vent to something he clearly felt strongly about.

At the end of his life, Debussy's music assumed more of a neo-classical quality as he forsook the symbolism and impressionism of his earlier work and embarked on a series of sonatas for various instrumental groups. In the event, only three of a planned six were completed: the **Cello Sonata** (1915), **Sonata for Flute, Viola and Harp** (1916) and **Violin Sonata** (1917). These works show Debussy employing a greater economy of structure and thematic organization which certainly suggest a new beginning, but also perhaps that the time of his most influential work was coming to an end.

STRAVINSKY

It was in Paris that Diaghilev, always on the lookout for new projects, suggested to Stravinsky, increasingly a presence in the city, a ballet based on some recently discovered fragments of music by the eighteenth century Italian composer Pergolesi. Sceptical at first, Stravinsky gradually warmed to the idea, perhaps sensing in this obscure but engaging music a way towards a new style of composition, related more to the European past than to the Russian folk song of which he was beginning to tire. At any rate, it was never going to be simply a case of making a conventional arrangement of the Pergolesi fragments, however much Diaghilev was, naively, expecting just that. Nevertheless, Stravinsky kept the melodic lines and bass parts largely intact, exercising his creativity on the harmony and orchestration which are subjected to some of his current compositional concerns: polychordal formations, added dissonances and unfamiliar instrumental combinations. These are done, however, with great subtlety and the uneducated ear can easily be fooled into thinking that it is hearing genuine eighteenth century music.

The new ballet, **Pulcinella**, occupied Stravinsky from 1919 to 1920 when it was first performed at the Paris Opéra. The public was delighted though the critics were, inevitably, more guarded, seeking to find a justification for Stravinsky's apparent act of musical terrorism. The composition of **Pulcinella** had the effect of opening a window onto the history of European music, signalling a change of direction for Stravinsky, one which would serve him for the next twenty five years.

Following the lead of **Pulcinella**, Stravinsky began an exploration of the past, specifically the textures, gestures and other characteristics associated with the various historical styles, but reinterpreting them, as previously noted, to give them a more contemporary flavor. Thus the running counterpoint of J.S.Bach provides the model for much of the instrumental fabric of the **Concerto for Piano and Wind Instruments** (1923–4, rev. 1950), whereas for his **Symphony in C** (1940), Stravinsky turned to the great Viennese classical masters, particularly Haydn and Beethoven, copies of whose works were on his desk as he composed. It is instructive to examine this score and observe Stravinsky sifting through the various ideas of his predecessors, selecting those which might be useful and modifying them to fit his own construction.

Although not acknowledged by Stravinsky, it has always seemed to this writer that the first movement of Mozart's **Symphony No. 40** lies behind some of the workings of Stravinsky's first movement. There is a strong resemblance between the string figurations and general texture used by Stravinsky at Figure 5 of his symphony and the opening of the Mozart with its divided violas. Similarly, it is perhaps not too fanciful to detect the example of the opening of Beethoven's **Seventh Symphony** in the rising scales supported by long, thematic notes which Stravinsky employs from Figure 3 onwards.

The cooler, more objective nature of this newer Stravinsky contrasts well with the earthy primitiveness of his earlier Russian period. But this is not, in fact, quite the radical departure that is often claimed. While happy recycling the patterns, devices and gestures found in older music, Stravinsky has no interest in coming to terms with the great unifying factor which gives it purpose and direction, namely tonality, with its complex network of harmonic relationships; a principle which

Stravinsky quite rightly felt had no relevance to the current situation. As before, then, we find harmonic functions banished in favor of a freer treatment of the diatonic materials and the responsibility for the forward momentum of the music given to rhythm.

Ex.9 Stravinsky, Symphony in C (coda to last movement)

© Copyright 1946 B. Schott's Söhne & Schott & Co, Ltd. © Copyright renewed 1976. Reproduced by permission. All rights reserved.

Stravinsky's solution to the problem of bringing the music to a close without the benefits of cadences was often to write a slow chorale-like passage where the harmonies revolve round each other before coming to rest. An early instance of this device can be found in the **Symphonies of Wind Instruments.** The **Symphony in C** contains a particularly beautiful, thematic example, the top note of the chords outlining the B,C,G motive on which the work is based, the chords themselves a subtle telescoping of tonic and dominant functions. The bass line cleverly creates an illusion of harmonic movement (Example 9).

Other instances include the ballet **Apollon musagete** (1928 rev.1947), the already-mentioned **Ebony Concerto** and the **Symphony of Psalms** (1930), its accompanying ostinato in successive 4ths contributing to a majestic and aurally stunning tapestry of sound.

LES SIX

Neo-classicism provided a welcome answer to the linguistic crisis of post-war European music and a viable alternative to Schoenberg's serialism. French composers, as we have suggested, were especially attracted to it, the way being led by the loosely knit group of friends known as Les Six whose members were Francis Poulenc (1899–1963), Darius Milhaud, Arthur Honegger (1892–1955), Germaine Tailleferre (1892–1983), Louis Durey (1888–1979) and Georges Auric (1899–1983). They had the good fortune to have the indefatigable writer and film maker Jean Cocteau (1889–1963) as their spokesman and promoter.

Cocteau's famous 1918 manifesto *Le coq et l'arlequin*, denouncing German art and advocating a general attitude of irreverence and frivolity, united Les Six and gave them a focus for their activities. Both they and Cocteau were further united by their love of Satie, whose own brand of irreverent wit elevated him to a position of spiritual godfather, but they also admired the neo-classical Stravinsky and were enthusiastic for the emerging popular culture. All these things combined were felt to be more representative of their era than the parallel modernism of Schoenberg and his followers.

Innovations in musical language were perhaps not as cataclysmic as those issuing from Vienna but that did not prevent novel and original ideas from appearing. Though not the first to be attracted to the possibilities of polytonality, Milhaud made extensive use of it and it has come to be associated with him. His ballet **Le bœuf sur le toit** (1919) contains some of the most characteristic examples. Milhaud's score is inspired by another favorite idiom – South American dance music, and the inclusion of polytonal passages gives a slightly comic tinge to the basically simple melodic and harmonic style of the music.

One striking novelty introduced by Milhaud is a speech-chorus, employed in his **Les choéphores** (1915), based on Aeschylus' Oresteia. In the sections leading up to Orestes' revenge killing of his mother Clytemnestra, and also at the end of the work, the narration is accompanied solely by percussion and the speech-chorus, the two treated as a single, equal entity with the chorus given rhythmicized shouts and other vocal effects – the first instance of its use in this way.

Eventually, however, having gained a certain *succès d'estime* with their 1921 collaborative venture **Les mariés de la tour Eiffel**, a piece of theatrical buffoonery, the group gradually began to lose momentum, an indication that they were not really a group in the strict sense, merely an assortment of like-minded friends. Cocteau referred to them all as a "movement." Honegger, for one, who had never properly worn the anti-Romantic badge which the group paraded, soon reverted to type, as is borne out by such deeply felt works as the oratorio **Jeanne d'Arc au bûcher** (1935–44) and the **Third Symphony ("Liturgique")** of 1945–46.

Of the others, the subsequent career of Poulenc is arguably the most fascinating. The various elements, listed above, which brought the group together in the first place remained with Poulenc, becoming subsumed into a highly refined and sophisticated style. The references in his neo-classicism chime with his own Gallic sensibility: Mozart, Saint-Saëns, Chabrier and, of course, Satie. Popular music was another source of inspiration, though jazz left him cold, and he was among those fascinated by the gamelan. He also showed a penchant for a charming, tongue-in-cheek sentimentality. In the **Concerto for Two Pianos** (1932), many of these influences come together and the way Poulenc glides effortlessly from one reference to another: mock-Mozart to sentimental ballad; gamelan to the music hall, is nothing short of miraculous. Poulenc's method is not so far removed from the all-inclusiveness of Mahler and Ives and strikingly anticipates the polystylism of later composers such as Schnittke.

In 1936 Poulenc underwent a reconversion to the Catholicism of his upbringing following the tragic death of his close friend and colleague Pierre-Octave Ferroud. This initiated a series of religious choral works, starting with the moving **Trois litanies à la vierge noire**, written after a pilgrimage to the shrine of the Black Virgin at Rocamadour in south-west France that same year. The aura of penitence in these works provides another dimension to the already wide ranging scope of Poulenc's art, though it could hardly diminish his natural ebullience and *bonhomie*, for it was not long before he produced **Les mamelles de Tirésias** (1939–44; rev. 1962)**,** a real *opéra bouffe* based on Apollinaire's farce about male-female role reversal. The serious and playful continued to live side by side in Poulenc.

By widening the terms of reference in their works, composers such as Poulenc and Stravinsky were undermining the narrowness of pure neo-classicism. Stravinsky went so far as to revisit the music of Tchaikovsky (an "expressive" composer if ever there was one) in the ballet **Le baiser de la fée** (1928) thereby going against the anti-romanticism which neo-classicism was supposed to be about. What we are witnessing here is not so much empty pastiche as a recognition that the music of other periods and cultures is available for further use and is still of great relevance. The borrowing and recycling of their stylistic features could be by turns, ironic, affectionate or satirical, depending on a composer's background and attitude, but the main point was a conscious engagement with the past, and to many artists active between the two world wars, this was not merely fashionable but expressive of a belief in survival through the continuation of tradition.

MUSIC OF SOCIAL CONSCIENCE

The serious application of neo-classical principles can be observed in much of the early music of the German Paul Hindemith (1895–1963). The impressive **Kammermusik** series, written between 1921 and 1928, shows Hindemith flexing his neo-classical muscles with an idiom featuring quasi-Baroque counterpoint and a driving, motoric rhythm. The harmonic system, though, is governed by Hindemith's unique compromise between tonality and twelve-note chromaticism.

Intervals are arranged along a gradient with the most consonant (octave, 4th and 5th) at one end and the most dissonant (minor 2nd and tritone) at the other. The preponderance of the purer intervals gives the music a distinctive, "open" quality that is immediately recognizable and it served Hindemith well in an output which, though not always so obviously neo-classical, was nevertheless rooted in the great classical past which Hindemith revered.

Hindemith was also a firm believer in the artist as a useful member of society, someone whose work, aimed at both amateur and professional, would enrich the lives of all who experienced it through the sheer pleasure of performance. This ideal, known in Germany as *Gebrauchsmusik* (literally, utility music), emphasized practicality as against what was seen as the Romantic, ivory tower view of art for art's sake and was an important side effect of the neo-classical movement, exerting considerable appeal during the 1930s.

In the case of Benjamin Britten, for instance, it helped to cement an already deeply held conviction that creative work must have a practical outcome. This need not imply compromise on the composer's part, nor need it suggest cultivating any particular way of writing. The composer can still be himself. Britten's consistency in this respect is shown as much in the way the voice of his long-term colleague and partner, the tenor Peter Pears, inspired a stream of wonderful songs, operatic roles and other vocal parts, as in his imaginative and fearless solutions to the problem of writing for children, giving them challenging music without writing down to them.

Britten's children's operas, **The Little Sweep** (1949) and **Noye's Fludde** (1957), are not particularly easy to perform but Britten is careful, as he always tried to be, to make every part, vocal or instrumental, lie within the performers' capabilities, or, to use his favorite expression, grateful.

Hindemith's indefatigable energy in the pursuit of his ideals produced an enormous number of compositions in every medium, including sonatas for every instrument. His educational music, from the prosaically titled **Educational Music for Instrumental Ensembles, Op.44** (1927), and the album of pieces **Music to Sing and Play** (1928) to the children's opera **Let's Build a Town** (1930), is also gratefully written and includes some novel ideas. Op.44 No.1 is a piece for strings written entirely in the first position and **Let's Build a Town** allows the performers to change the score or add bits of their own as required.

Despite their down-to-earth practicality, Hindemith and Britten were not above addressing serious social, moral or ethical subjects in their work. The moving story of the sixteenth century painter, Mathias Grűnewald, and his struggle against intolerance, as told in Hindemith's opera **Mathis der Maler** (1933–5), was seen by its composer to be an exact parallel to the contemporary artist's situation.

A social conscience of a similar kind led Michael Tippett (1905–1998) to create the oratorio **A Child of our Time** (1939–41). The success of this work is due in no small part to its relation to the English choral tradition (though Tippett's model was J.S. Bach's settings of the Passions), but the inspired insertion of Negro Spirituals where Bach would have used chorales provides that necessary 'common touch' which Hindemith's opera lacks. (It is significant that the

Symphony – Mathis der Maler (1934), the four movements of which were originally intended as orchestral interludes in the opera, has been far more successful.) As with Britten, neither Hindemith nor Tippett felt the need to change their styles in any way to accommodate the subject matter they were dealing with, though Hindemith was beginning to experience problems as the emerging Nazi party exerted their squeeze on the modern movement in the arts. He eventually succumbed to the pressure and was forced to leave, like so many others, for the relative safety of America.

For Tippett, the Nazi threat, though real enough, was still hundreds of miles away, and his reactions to events in the world could only be vicarious. Tippett's own attitude to such matters was (and continued to be) to use his powers as a creative artist to give people positive images of hope. But for those closer to the action, things were a lot different, as many German artists knew only too well. If they were also Jewish, their predicament was even greater.

WEILL

The case of Kurt Weill (1900–50) is typical. In the late 1920s, Weill began collaborating with the playwright Bertolt Brecht (1898–1956), a move that necessitated abandoning the extended-tonal, late Romantic idiom of his earlier work in favor of one that would match Brecht's epic drama and its concept of the alienation of the spectator from the events on stage. Weill's instinct was perfect: a music derived from the song style of the Berlin cabaret, *oom-pah* accompaniments and all, but with harmonic progressions designed to avoid sentimentality and predictability. It is a subtle art, heard at its best in the **Mahagonny**

Songspiel (1927) and **The Threepenny Opera** (1928), but it caught exactly Brecht's caustic wit, base humor and relentless mockery of the social nightmare of the Weimar Republic.

But an art of social protest was untenable for a Jewish artist in 1930s Germany and Weill was forced to join the exodus to America. Once there, he adapted his new style for the Broadway stage, a move for which he has received a fair amount of not altogether unjustified criticism. It is obvious that his Berlin style could not translate intact to Broadway, being, as it were, site- and time-specific, but Weill was also unable to match its originality, and his Broadway songs, even at their best (**Speak Low, My Ship, September Song**), are largely indistinguishable from those of other composers working in the genre.

RUSSIA

One composer who personifies the victimization of the artist at the hands of a totalitarian regime is Dmitri Shostakovich. Russia under Stalin was comparable to Germany under the Nazis. The job of purging the country of modernist, progressive tendencies, (the official term there was 'formalist'), which were seen as symbols of Western degeneracy and decadence, was just as brutal and its effect decisive.

By 1936, the year that *Pravda* published its notorious denunciation of Shostakovich's opera **Lady Macbeth of Mtsensk** (1930–32), which had just enjoyed two years of public success since its Leningrad premiere in 1934, the composer's career as a modernist was more or less over. He finished his **Fourth Symphony** the year of the *Pravda* article but withdrew it before the intended premiere, fearing, justifiably, that the work's high level of dissonance and rather wild inventiveness would invite more trouble from the authorities. Thereafter the style was toned down and, despite some magnificent, anguished music, the old fire was never rekindled.

Most Russian composers were, in fact, walking this tightrope, trying to balance a desire to be part of the progressive West while simultaneously appealing to the mass of ordinary listeners. Prokofiev was one such composer. A natural penchant for experiment was, fortunately for him, balanced by an alluring, even Romantic, lyricism but the combination did not always wash with the Soviet authorities. Prokofiev's belief in innovation through tradition was not shared by them, for innovation was regarded as having no place in an art of and for the people.

AMERICA

Changes of direction might be the result of external pressures but might equally come from a composer's taking stock of his own position with regard to simply making a success of his career. Such was the motivation behind the American composer Aaron Copland's realization in the 1930s that success with a larger audience might come if he could communicate his ideas in a more direct and simple manner. Copland (1900–1990) had already achieved a certain notoriety with a style that combined two of his prime concerns at the time: European modernism and American jazz. Copland had become familiar with the former during his stay in Paris during the 1920s where he had been one of the pupils of Nadia Boulanger. Her championing of the neo-classical Stravinsky was particularly crucial for Copland, who must have found there the same sort of rhythmic drive and excitement that existed in jazz. But the integration of the two elements proved problematic.

There is a wide gulf separating the jazz-inspired **Piano Concerto** of 1926 with the serialist **Piano Variations** of 1930, such that they could almost be from the pens of two different composers. The **Piano Variations** is a confident and assured piece of writing and the four-note cell on which it is largely based is deployed with an imagination and rigor which is truly impressive.

The **Piano Concerto**, on the other hand, is feeble in comparison, the jazz element failing to lift the piece above the superficial. In this respect, Copland's understanding of jazz is markedly inferior to that of his friend Darius Milhaud, whose **La création du monde** is discussed above.[11] On the other hand, Copland's 1948 **Clarinet Concerto,** written for Benny Goodman (1909–86), is far more successful. Clearly, the liquid elegance, as well as the infectious drive, of Goodman's playing inspired Copland to create a solo part which is idiomatic and at the same time sits happily in the concerto format.

But a new attitude took over during the 1930s and Copland began to unveil a more overtly "populist" style in a series of works on specifically American themes, ranging from the ballets **Rodeo** (1938) and **Appalachian Spring** (1943–45) to the character piece **El salón México** (1932–6) with its evocative use of Latin American rhythms and colors. Several successful film scores also date from this period. With these works, Copland aligned himself to the European *Gebrauchsmusik* movement and at the same time achieved a genuine American nationalism, very different from the transcendentalism of Ives, yet owing much to his bold integration of the serious and popular.

It seemed at the time that this new side of Copland might obliterate the former but he never lost the desire to write for a more 'highbrow' audience, as is made evident by such works as **Connotations** (1962) and **Inscape** (1967), which use a modified serial technique. But there are other instances of an attempt at a synthesis of the two sides, as for example in his **Music for a Great City** (1964).

The style here is angular, dissonant and brash, with nods towards the rhythmic excitement of jazz, evoking the noisy cityscape of the composer's native New York (though the work was commissioned by the London Symphony Orchestra). In a sense, Copland is continuing on the path indicated by the 'symphonic' Gershwin, but the kindred spirit of Leonard Bernstein (1918–1990), one of Copland's greatest admirers and interpreters, is also not far away.

Copland's achievements in embracing the musical vernacular are by no means unique to him though the brash confidence and easy appeal of the music has tended to overshadow the not always inferior contributions of some of his colleagues. Roy Harris (1898–1979) and Virgil Thomson (1896–1989) both tried, in their different ways, to establish a distinctively American style from a basically neo-classical standpoint. Harris's **Third Symphony** (1938) has always been held up as a paradigm of American forthrightness and for sheer rhythmic drive and energy it is the equal of any of Copland's scores. Thomson's reductive, simple style, derived from his admiration for Satie, is not dissimilar to that of the Copland of **Appalachian Spring**. Perhaps, though, Harris and Thomson lack the 'common touch' that came naturally to Copland.

Sibelius and Nielsen

Thus, a movement which started out as a defiant gesture of anti-Romanticism softened up, its irony and cynicism rendered ineffectual with the passing of the 1920s, to be subsumed under an anti-modernist conservatism. For, despite the comings and goings of various avant-gardes, there still remained, and continues to remain, a remarkable faithfulness to the old nineteenth century symphonic and expressive tradition. The hold that the symphony has continued to exert over a good number of composers during the increasingly fragmented twentieth century is an indication that the large-scale working out of ideas has never lost its relevance.

Some of the greatest contributions to the symphony and symphonic form have been made, to be sure, by composers born, as it were, into the tradition. The imposing Scandinavian pair, Jean Sibelius (1865–1957) and Carl Nielsen (1865–1931), grew up at the height of the symphony's development and it stayed central to their work.

Sibelius's seven essays in the medium show a gradual mastery of the art of organic growth through motivic integration, achieved with a tonal language which is surprisingly simple yet completely unmistakeable and individualistic. The culmination of his method is the mighty **Seventh Symphony** of 1924, an utterly compelling demonstration of how to telescope the structure's traditional four movements into one unbroken span.

Nielsen, by contrast, favored a more extrovert, Romantic style, consistent with the dynamic positivism of his personal philosophy. This manifested itself in an equally individualistic language and approach to tonality in which the main key of a piece emerges only at the end after a long struggle, a method dubbed "progressive tonality."[12]

Sibelius and Nielsen belong, temperamentally, to an older tradition and neither was seriously affected by the radical changes in the musical landscape of the first quarter of the twentieth century. Sibelius, in fact, gave up composing altogether, having tried and failed to complete an eighth symphony.

Nielsen's awareness of what was happening is reflected in his **Sixth Symphony (Sinfonia semplice)** (1924–5), his last, where he makes some feeble attempts to poke fun at what he perceived as threats to the stability of the great symphonic tradition which he had been at great pains to keep alive and viable. Coming on the heels of his powerful **Fifth Symphony** (1922), one of the greatest and most original in the repertoire, the Sixth is a huge disappointment and an anti-climax to a symphonic career of enormous stature.

PART 2:
AFTER 1945

1
A Fresh Beginning

With the century not yet half way through, the variety, complexity and changeability of twentieth century music, referred to at the beginning of Part 1, is already a fact of life, though, with the benefit of hindsight, it is possible to see a pattern emerging. John Cage once rather glibly asserted that the choice for a young composer was whether to follow Schoenberg or Stravinsky i.e. serialism or neo-classicism, and to many composers these two figures, while not exactly acting out a modern *guerre des bouffons,* had come to represent the two principal faces of modernism, with the former the more radical. This is an oversimplification, of course, but, with the American experimental movement still in its infancy and the Futurists scoring only limited success, the concept is broadly accurate. The real issue revolves around language, specifically attitudes towards tonality. The overthrowing of this venerable old system is actually not as widespread as is often believed. Serialism and free atonality had limited currency (Webern was hardly known before 1945) whereas a large number of composers remained committed to some form of tonal organization.

Messiaen

Around the time of the Second World War, the musical universe began to experience more upheaval as the combined forces of accelerated technological progress and disillusionment with radical social change helped to foster among artists a need to start all over again, as though everything accomplished since the dawn of the century had been in vain. To some young composers, this meant the virtual reinvention of music, and it so happened that a number of forces were in place to make this possible.

A key figure here was Olivier Messiaen (1908–92), a French composer with one of the most distinctive voices of the twentieth, or indeed any other, century, but also a highly influential teacher of wide-ranging sympathies. His inclination towards modality, harmony as color and the exotic and mystical made him the natural heir to Debussy and his direction as a composer was clarified during the 30s and 40s as he gradually assimilated the curious blend of influences that would make up his unique language.

His melodic style is based on the contours of Gregorian chant, Indian music and, famously, birdsong, while his harmony is derived from a group of synthetic modes. The peculiar characteristics of these modes, with their symmetrical arrangements of intervals, allows them to be transposed only a limited number of times, hence their description as "modes of limited transposition." Messiaen regarded the modes as possessing color properties, a result of his highly developed synaesthesia, and, by combining their notes in different ways, he could suggest different shades. Example 10 shows the second mode (a) and Messiaen's method of extracting unusual chords (b), taken from his treatise **The Technique of my Musical Language**.

Ex.10(a)   Messiaen, Second mode of limited transposition

Ex.10(b)   Messiaen, Characteristic chords derived from 2nd mode

Reproduced by permission of Editions Alphonse Leduc, Paris/United Music Publishers Ltd.

It was, however, in the field of rhythm that Messiaen made his most original contribution. Again, Indian music provided the main source, in this case the collection of 120 rhythmic patterns, or 'deçi-tâlas', which were compiled by the medieval Indian theorist, Sharngadeva.[13] Messiaen subjects these rhythms to all manner of variation and development, for example the augmentation and diminution of entire rhythms or single values from them, adding extra values, retrograding them, and so on. Much of the inspiration for this comes from Stravinsky's innovatory procedures in the final part, the Sacrificial Dance, of **The Rite of Spring**, but Messiaen goes much further. In his music, rhythm becomes completely liberated from melody and harmony, and indeed pulse, concerning itself purely with its own characteristics – duration and number.

One outcome of this is that Messiaen can use the abstract nature of rhythm to symbolize some of the extra-musical concerns which are important to him as a composer. Above all, Messiaen was a devout Catholic, but one with strong mystical leanings, and almost all his music is an expression of his faith. If his modality and associated harmony expressed the colors and sensations of the physical world, then rhythm expressed more abstract concepts such as eternity and the flow of time. Eternity could be expressed, for instance, by a rhythmic palindrome, a non-retrogradable rhythm in Messiaen's own terminology, which suggests a circular motion, or alternatively by a series of progressively longer durations, stretching, by implication, to infinity.

In terms of structure, Messiaen preferred the juxtaposition of discrete blocks of contrasting material rather than the continuous, dynamic narrative of the older, symphonic tradition. Development of material was eschewed in favor of repetition and variation, a procedure again found in early Stravinsky, particularly works like the **Symphonies of Wind Instruments.**

A characteristic example of Messiaen's method is the 1963 **Couleurs de la cité céleste**, a work for wind instruments, percussion and piano which simply alternates sections based on three types of material: birdsong, plainchant and color-harmonies. These latter, often supplied with the actual names of the colors envisaged by the composer, are created by superimposing one chord onto another, each with its own instrumentation, creating what Messiaen calls 'added resonance'. Example 11 shows three complex chords on clarinets, trumpets and trombones, each then modified by a second chord on horns, trombone, piano, tuned cowbell and the added color of a gong. Of particular note are the various dynamic levels within the sound. Messiaen's color description is included for good measure.

Ex.11 Messiaen, Couleurs de la cité céleste (fig.18)

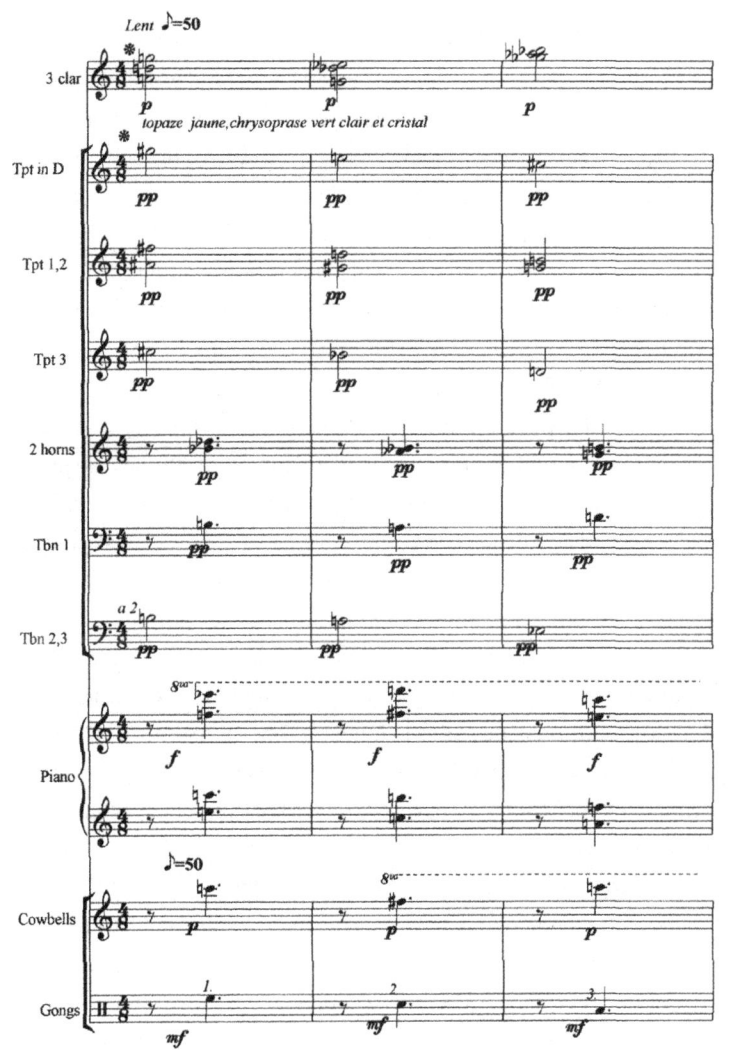

※ Ici: la couleur principale et la fond de la musique sont aux cuivres- les clarinettes restent aux second plan

Reproduced by permission of Editions Alphonse Leduc, Paris/United Music Publishers Ltd

Messiaen's Influence

Messiaen's influence began to have an effect as early as the 1940s when he was teaching at the Paris Conservatoire and working on major projects like the 10-movement **Turangalîla-Symphonie** (1946–8), one of a number of compositions which marked the end of his early maturity. In 1949, Messiaen embarked on a series of largely experimental works which feature techniques derived from serial procedures including much use of permutations of 12 note series and groups of durations. Messiaen's way with this material is highly abstract, even cerebral and, it need hardly be added, utterly different from what Schoenberg, Berg and even Webern had been doing.

Messiaen would stimulate the imaginations of his students by introducing them to these radical ideas. In one of his classes, he posited a further modification of serial technique. This was the suggestion that the principles of serialism need not be confined solely to the organisation of pitch, as Schoenberg and his pupils had done, but might be extended to include the other parameters of sound, such as duration, loudness or timbre. In order to demonstrate this, Messiaen produced, in 1949, a piano piece with the cumbersome title **Mode de valeurs et d'intensités** ("Mode of durations and volume levels"). The term 'mode' is roughly equivalent to 'series' but Messiaen has devised several "modes" by separating the four (not two) basic characteristics of piano sound, namely duration and volume level plus pitch and type of attack. Moreover, there are three series of pitches, occupying the top, middle and low registers of the piano and overlapping each other, and each of these has its own series of durations which augment incrementally; the first in demisemiquavers, the second in semiquavers, the third in quavers.

It is clear that Messiaen's treatment of these materials is much more influenced by his own modal inclinations than by the serialism of the Second Viennese School. It is also important to stress that Messiaen wrote this piece to demonstrate how the different parameters of sound *might* be organized. As far as he was concerned, that was the end of the matter and he never followed up the implications.

Judged purely as a piece of music, the **Mode de valeurs et d'intensités** is not particularly interesting, but it had one novel element: every note had its own duration, dynamic level, pitch and type of attack – it existed in its own private world, as it were. When Messiaen played the work to a group of his students on the summer school at Darmstadt in 1951, he could not have realized what he was setting in motion. Two of the students were completely bowled over by the piece and it literally changed their lives overnight. The students were Pierre Boulez (b.1925) and Karlheinz Stockhausen (1928–2007) and they both saw in the piece pointers to a new type of music, one where every aspect of sound, its parameters, could be pre-determined by applying the principle of serialism to them. There was also a connection with certain characteristics in the late music of Webern, which was just beginning to be known.

If composers were to start again, the way forward was being suggested by both Messiaen and Webern. A totally pre-determined music also meant, of course, that the performer would simply perform and not get involved with 'interpretation'. This would put the final nail in the romantic coffin and pretty much sever all ties with music's past.

INTEGRAL SERIALISM

The appeal of all this to radical young minds in the 1950s is not hard to imagine. The Darmstadt summer school became the Mecca for young European-based composers who included, in addition to Boulez and Stockhausen, Luigi Nono (1924–90), Luigi Dallapiccola (1904–75), Bruno Maderna (1920–73), and Henri Pousseur (b.1929). (In America,

Milton Babbitt was working with similar ideas though producing rather different results.) In Darmstadt, composers could listen to each others' works, attend each others' lectures and exchange ideas. The effect on Boulez was nothing short of cataclysmic, as, with all the zeal of a religious convert, he began his now notorious castigation of the past, urging the destruction of all opera houses and pledging his faith in the holy doctrine of total serialism as the only possible language of the future. For this reason, Boulez held up Webern as the model to follow; Schoenberg was too tied to the romantic tradition, as indeed was Messiaen. (At that time, Messiaen wryly observed, Boulez was 'against everything'.)

BOULEZ AND STOCKHAUSEN

The goal of total (or integral) serialism was quickly achieved. Boulez chose, not surprisingly, the monochromatic sound of two pianos, rather than the more "expressive" winds or strings, for his first essay, **Structures 1** (1951), whose very title is an advertisement for the new aesthetic. Ironically, Boulez' pitch series is that of Messiaen's first pitch mode in the **Mode de Valeurs et d'Intensités** but whereas Messiaen, despite the individualisation of every note, keeps a sense of linear continuity, Boulez emphasises the notes' individualities by separating them from each other, largely by extreme changes of register, or at most grouping a few notes together in a kind of jagged gesture. This actually gives the music an unpredictable quality, totally at odds with the control of materials that the composer is exercising. For the moment, however, the discontinuity of texture was precisely what Boulez wanted.

The weakness of the **Structures** lies in the academic rigor with which Boulez applies the serial principle, laying the piece open to easy analysis as though it were a textbook example. To be fair, though, Boulez was attracted by the *technique* of integral serialism and the new language that could be created with it. It was a bold step into a radically new concept of composition and there is an unmistakable aggressiveness in the **Structures** which seems to be calling attention to the brave new world on display.

How instructive it is to compare Boulez' effort with that of his colleague Stockhausen. For him, the total control of sound was the key to a new, imaginative sound-world, one which would increasingly have magical qualities. Stockhausen's first foray with the new technique was a chamber work for oboe, bass clarinet, piano and 3 percussionists. It also dates from 1951 and it illustrates the extraordinary range of Stockhausen's imagination as well as his refusal to submit to any form of dogma. Its title, **Kreuzspiel** ("crossplay"), refers to the way Stockhausen utilizes the serial principle, whereby an initial note-row Eb-Db-C-D-Bb-F-B-E-G-A-Ab-Gb is permutated 12 times until it appears as B-E-G-A-Ab-Gb-Eb-Db-C-D-Bb-F; in other words the two hexachords change positions. Each pitch has its own duration, the resulting duration-series likewise permutating. This basic idea of a structure in which individual elements move from one position to another is applied to the piece in different ways and on different levels.

Furthermore, Stockhausen assigns the instruments different roles; the three pitched instruments, for example, operate for the most part in restricted ranges: piano in the extreme treble and bass, with the oboe and bass clarinet medium high and medium low respectively. Thus, alongside the serial treatment of pitch, duration and dynamics, Stockhausen gives structural significance to timbre and register as well.[14]

Both Boulez and Stockhausen continued to wrestle with the demands of integral serialism throughout the 1950s. Employing all manner of complex manipulations and permutations on the basic material, they gained entrance to a world of sound relationships held together by ever more arcane and abstract methods of organization. One result might be a masterpiece of fragile beauty like Boulez' **Le marteau sans maître** (1953–5), in many ways a typical product of the times, with its exotic scoring for alto voice, alto flute, guitar, viola, vibraphone, xylorimba and percussion, all of which, voice included, are given equal status and exactly the same type of angular music.

But the level of virtuosity required to perform **Le marteau sans maître,** high though it is, is as nothing compared with that of the

Stockhausen **Klavierstücke**, the group of extraordinary piano pieces he began in 1952, which really demand a new breed of interpreter. The first piece (actually written in 1953) calls for different subdivisions of the bar to be played simultaneously and, at one point, a nine-note chord containing six different dynamic levels (Example 12).

Ex.12 Stockhausen, Piano Piece 1, bar 53

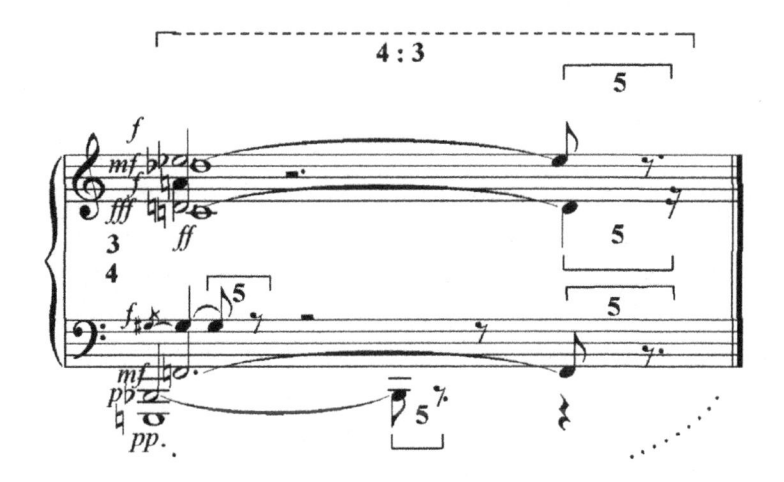

© Copyright 1954 by Universal Edition (London) Ltd, London. Reproduced by permission. All rights reserved.

The formidable difficulties thrown up by the methodology of integral serialism were a barrier to many performers, but to Stockhausen they were all part of what was becoming a journey of discovery into the nature of sound itself: what it consisted of and how we perceive it. Stockhausen's researches were typically wide and thorough but he was also particularly fortunate to be in at the start of one of the century's major breakthroughs.

Musique Concrète and Electronic Music

A desire to invent new instruments had for years been voiced by certain forward-looking composers, notably Busoni and Varèse, and a degree of success had been achieved by the harnessing of electricity for the purpose. Of these new instruments, only the ondes Martenot, a keyboard instrument capable of a siren-like glissando over its entire range, and possessing a powerful, shrieking, if somewhat sickly, sound, found any sort of acceptance, largely in France. Important parts for it were included by Messiaen in some of his scores, most notably the **Turangalîla-Symphonie**.

Varèse, however, had visualized a radically new type of music but the means to achieve this were not really forthcoming until the invention of the tape recorder during the 1930s. The full potential of this machine was not realized until the late 1940s when it was found to be the perfect tool for some new ideas being hatched in the studios of French Radio (R.T.F.) in Paris. These involved the composition of short, collage-like pieces made entirely with sounds from the natural world, both outside the studio (machines, animals, the weather) and inside (hitting, scraping, rubbing, etc. whatever objects were to hand).

This new music became known as *musique concrète* and the invention of the tape recorder enabled the composer not only to record the sounds easily but also, thanks to the malleability of the tape, to transform them by various techniques of editing. It was easy to turn a tape over and play it backwards and machines could run at different speeds. This latter function had an added attraction: a recorded sound played back twice as fast would also appear an octave higher, one twice as slow an octave lower. The replaying and re-recording of different sounds simultaneously allowed for the creation of complex textures, a technique known as montage.

Most exciting of all, the tape could be cut and rejoined (spliced), giving the composer the ability to create not only unheard-of sequences of sounds but also to change the internal organization of a sound. The initial crash of a wave breaking on the shore could be cut out and put back in the middle of the sound of the water ebbing. It could also be replaced by something else, and so on.

The first piece of *musique concrète*, the **Etude aux chemins de fer** (Study in Railways), was made in 1948 by Pierre Schaeffer (1910–95), then a technician at the studios of French Radio. One should not underestimate the amazingly bold leap of imagination into the unknown exercised by Schaeffer and the young composers who were attracted to the studios by his pioneering work – Pierre Henry, Bernard Parmegiani (both b.1927), Luc Ferrari (b.1929), François Bayle (b.1932) – for, despite the naive qualities of much of their output, the acceptance of noise as "musical" sound and the creative use of technology were liberating elements in music's evolution during the twentieth century and some of the best pieces, Bayle's **Trois rêves d'oiseaux** (1963–71), to name but one, are genuinely moving.

The almost parallel development on the other side of the Rhine of using tape to record and manipulate electronic sound is a further indication that a new threshold was being crossed. The studio of the West German Radio (WDR) at Cologne under the direction of Herbert Eimert (1897–1972) became host to the first compositions of pure electronic music which include the two **Studien** by Stockhausen (1953 and 1954), made exclusively from electronically generated sine tones (pure tones without harmonics). These are complex works, organized by serially derived techniques and are a noticeable contrast to the examples of *musique concrète*, composed largely intuitively.

Inevitably, the resources of electronic music and *musique concrète* were merged to form what is generally called electro-acoustic music (though other terms, such as 'acousmatic', are often encountered) and, again, Stockhausen was at the forefront of developments. His **Gesang der Jünglinge** (1955–6), though obviously an early example of this new genre, shows a remarkable maturity in the boldness of its conception and its technical assurance. One novel feature is the way Stockhausen applies serial control to the points in space from where the sounds emanate – in other words, the positioning of the loudspeakers. Stockhausen also foresees a future development by having his two sound-sources, a boy's voice and electronic sound, not just co-exist, but take on each other's characteristics. Thus the intensive research into sound conducted by Stockhausen quickly bore fruit.

Shortly after this, Varèse produced his **Poème électronique**, referred to above, which was designed to be heard while walking round the specially built pavilion for the Philips Company at the 1958 Brussels World Fair. Varèse had finally realized his dream but was never able to repeat the achievement.

The subsequent development of electro-acoustic music has been a troubled one. Following the example of the WDR studio at Cologne, others were quickly established in radio stations and, especially, in universities throughout Europe and the United States. This proliferation of studios was matched by a rapid increase in the sophistication of equipment, firstly through miniaturization as valves gave way to transistors and printed circuits (and ultimately to computers and digital control), and secondly through the development of more and more ways of transforming basic sounds, the starting point for this type of composition.

An inevitable and serious knock-on effect of this latter aspect was that it became difficult to avoid a composition sounding like a demonstration of some technical procedure or other. On the other hand, as in the best contrapuntal music of the seventeenth and eighteenth centuries, technical excellence plus imagination can produce artistic results of high quality and there are numerous examples of electro-acoustic works which fulfil these criteria, if one can get to experience them.

The reception of electro-acoustic music in the public domain has, however, been mostly unfavorable so that what seemed, in the 1960s, to be the beginning of an exciting new chapter in the story of twentieth century music, turned out to be something of a damp squib. The "inhuman" nature of electronic sound and the absence of visual stimuli in concerts of tape pieces (an aspect which will be returned to later) may be minus points but there is also no doubt that the appropriation of the technology (and in some cases, even the language) by composers and producers of commercial and popular music biassed opinion against the more "classical" fraternity, the difference between the two camps being then exacerbated by marketing.

THE DARMSTADT LEGACY

The 1950s were an astonishingly fertile period, not only for Stockhausen, who seemed to be everywhere and doing everything, but for all those who, inspired by the activities at Darmstadt, were engaged in the re-invention of music. Integral serialism was only one development and it was by no means widely used, though the angular, unpredictable nature of its sound-world did influence that of other, more freely organized music. But the period was particularly notable, even notorious, for the production of scores of the utmost complexity as composers fought to outdo each other in the invention of musical structures, the various elements of which being interconnected in ever more abstract and fanciful ways. Program notes accompanying performances of such works were often equally as abstruse.

More productive, however, were the explorations of music's relationship with language and the visual, theatrical nature of performance. The former remained a special preoccupation of Luciano Berio (1925–2003) since the composition of his **Thema (Omaggio a Joyce)** in 1958, a tape piece which resulted from intensive analysis of vocal sound in the Studio di Fonologia Musicale in Milan (which Berio co-founded with Bruno Maderna) and his meeting with the extraordinary vocal artist, Cathy Berberian (1925–83). The words of the text of **Thema** (from James Joyce's *Ulysses*) are treated as though they were musical sounds, the composition blurring the distinction between words and music.

THEATER

Exploitation of the theatrical side of performance is largely a reflection of the increasing cross-fertilization between different genres which began to occupy the attention of many artists during this period. As early as 1952, John Cage had organized a special event at Black Mountain College, North Carolina, which consisted of himself and several of his friends performing different activities simultaneously. Thus Cage read one of his lectures, David Tudor played the piano, Merce Cunningham danced, paintings and slides were shown. This now famous event is generally considered the prototype of the "happening", that typical product of 1960s crossover. It was certainly a sign of the way the American avant-garde was heading, spawning a whole movement of multi-media performances as well as elevating the visual side of performance to the same level as the sound. The Fluxus artists (of whom more later) were an important part of this movement.

The Argentinian-born but German-based Mauricio Kagel (1931–2008) has made many notable contributions to this genre, among them the "percussion" piece **Pas de cinq** (1965). The five percussionists, individually attired, create a rhythmic polyphony by walking in different ways at different speeds on a specially prepared "set" of surfaces made of various materials. Walking sticks are used to increase the rhythmic complexity. **Pas de cinq** is a splendid example of Kagel's theatrical manner, by turns ironic, surreal or just plain funny. Other, more straightforwardly, visual pieces include the highly entertaining **Match** (1964) for two duelling virtuoso cellists and a percussionist-referee.

A slightly different aspect of the visual dimension is in the field of electro-acoustic music where there is a minimum of visual interest; just the equipment and perhaps one or two people operating it. This rather barren spectacle led to various experiments with multi-loudspeaker arrangements where their positioning and the space between enhance the listening experience by the composer (or operator) having the sounds travel from one location to another. The final stage was the creation of what is generally referred to as live electronic music, where the equipment for making tape pieces is transferred from studio to concert hall and performed on live. Often, though, instrumentalists and vocalists were included, playing acoustically against the electro-acoustic backdrop or having their sound modified by playing into microphones connected to the equipment.

The experience with multi-speaker electro-acoustic music was crucial for composers like Stockhausen, who soon found a way of translating the technique into purely instrumental terms. His **Gruppen** (1957) is scored for three orchestras, each with its own conductor, placed on three sides of the concert hall. Stockhausen devises many ways to make the three orchestras interact and the audience's experience will vary according to their seating positions.

A grandiose development of this idea can be seen in his ambitious **Sternklang** (Star-sound), conceived for open-air performance and completed in 1971, which uses five quartets of amplified though unspecified instruments/voices (roughly S.A.T.B.), widely separated (typically about 70 metres from each other) and grouped round a central percussionist. The pitch material is made to fluctuate and revolve round the performance area. This material comprises five 8-note chords, pitches 2 to 9 of the harmonic series on the five fundamentals C, D, E, F# and A. The chords have one note, the E above middle C, in common and this acts as a kind of tonal center, the harmonies revolving round it in different degrees of density, creating the "Star-sound". (It is also the pitch of the central percussionist's tubular bell.)

One of the many features of **Sternklang** is the transporting of musical material by the performers from one group to another. The idea of having performers move while they play or sing had been a feature of John Cage's experimental works of the 50s and was taken up by several composers, an early and celebrated instance being Berio's **Circles** (1960), written for Berberian, where the vocalist moves in a circle round the performance area delineated by the accompanying percussion and harp.

Music Theater in England

These works helped to create the genre known as music theater, a genre which could encompass experimental works like those of Berio and Kagel described above, which is theater in its widest sense, as well as works more obviously related to a "normal" theatrical tradition, and all stages in between. In England, Harrison Birtwistle and Peter Maxwell Davies (both b.1934) were particularly attracted to the genre. Davies's point of departure was Schoenberg's **Pierrot lunaire**, a work towards whose dark expressionism and use of Sprechgesang Davies had a particular affinity.

It stimulated him and Birtwistle to found the Pierrot Players (later renamed the Fires of London) in order to perform their new works alongside Schoenberg's masterpiece. Thus came into being such adventurous works as Davies' **Eight Songs for a Mad King** (1969) which features a manic, hysterical vocal part (the mad King George III) and instrumentalists who perform in separate cages, representing the birds he allegedly tried to teach to sing.

Birtwistle's inspiration came largely from English folk myths and Greek drama. These two sources have been responsible not only for the impressive and highly varied series of operas he has produced, from the small-scale **Punch and Judy** (1966–7) through to the more ambitious **The Mask of Orpheus** (1973–83), with its inclusion of electronic tapes, but also to a large part of his instrumental output.

Birtwistle, in fact, views composition as a dramatic process and performance as theater, in the sense of the players acting out some kind of ritual. In **Tragoedia** (1965), the 10-piece ensemble is divided into three groups – string quartet, wind quintet and harp – and are made to articulate the formal structure of ancient Greek tragedy. In other works, the theatrical aspect is more hidden, as in the aptly-named **Secret Theater** (1984).

THE MIDDLE AGES REVISITED

Maxwell Davies and Birtwistle were also leading players in the upsurge of interest in medieval and renaissance music (now generally referred to as 'early music') that occurred in England during the post-war years. This perhaps unexpected movement within the avant-garde has been variously explained as a desire to establish a continuity between the young modernist composer and his past which would bypass the folk-revivalists and acknowledge recent developments in European music; as a flight from the European classical tradition into a world which was, at that time, largely unfamiliar and therefore safe from critical judgement; as a realization that there was a similarity between the techniques employed by medieval and renaissance composers and those of the post-war serialists.

However true the first two explanations are, there is little doubt that the third was much more to the point. Davies and Birtwistle, along with Alexander Goehr (b.1932), fellow students at the Royal Manchester College of Music (now the Royal Northern College of Music) were in fact among the first composers in England to be actively interested in and influenced by the European avant-garde (Messiaen, Boulez, Stockhausen et al.), and also *their* predecessors: Stravinsky, Schoenberg and Webern.

The attraction of medieval and renaissance music to these young composers lay in the abstract and arcane nature of some of the techniques employed. Of particular fascination was isorhythm, where a repeated rhythmic pattern of a certain length (the *talea*) is superimposed onto a repeated melodic pattern (the *color*) of a different length. Depending on their respective lengths, the beginnings of the two patterns will coincide every so often. Isorhythm is thus a useful tool for achieving continuity and its general principle of two structural units moving in the same direction but independently is capable of being adapted to suit differing purposes and schemes. A relatively straightforward usage may be found in Birtwistle's chamber piece **La plage: Eight Songs of Remembrance** (1972) whereas a greatly expanded version of the principle informs his huge orchestral work **The Triumph of Time** (1971–2).

Maxwell Davies's indebtedness to medieval music is apparent in his obsessive use of plainchant melodies as pitch material, these also providing the titles of the works (thus **Alma redemptoris mater** (1957) and **Ave maris stella** (1975)). Fragments drawn from these melodies (usually the first few notes) are Davies's alternative to a note-row and they are subjected to a variety of transformations derived from both serial and medieval techniques. For example, the different intervals which make up a given plainchant fragment may be allotted different rhythmic cells or duration values, expressed as ratios (thus dotted minim + crotchet equates to a ratio of 3:1), these becoming the building blocks for further elaboration.

Davies has also made extensive use of permutation and rotation techniques but on rather novel lines, typically organizing a set of permutated pitches and/or rhythmic cells into magic squares in order to create more connections. Birtwistle, on the other hand, prefers to use tables of random numbers as a means of introducing 'impurities' into rigorously controlled procedures.

INDETERMINACY, CHANCE AND ALEATORICISM

In 1957 and 1958, John Cage made two visits to the Darmstadt Summer School, events which threw this already exhilarating gathering of minds into even greater turmoil. Cage, it will be recalled, had arrived at a critical point in his career; the embracing of noise and silence, plus the contact with Zen, were moving him further away from the traditional concerns of western art.

This distancing would, moreover, be sharpened by two other discoveries: firstly, that silence did not really exist – it was filled with all manner of sound, what Cage came to refer to as unintentional sound (the celebrated "silent" piece, **4'33"** (1952) is simply an invitation for us to listen to this unintentional sound); secondly, the ancient Chinese oracle the I Ching, or Book of Changes. This venerable old text is a way of obtaining advice by a chance mechanism, the simplest being the tossing of coins. Cage's introduction to the book was the final thing he was looking for.

By a simple adaptation, he could use the oracle to obtain answers to all questions pertaining to a particular composition, replacing his own choices with those given by chance. He would have to accept whatever was thrown up by chance, of course, but this chimed perfectly with his new sympathies.

Cage's first tentative steps with the I Ching nevertheless produced one major composition, the **Music of Changes** (1951), a large scale work for solo piano where the I Ching was used to organize a succession of sound events, from single notes to more complex groupings, including their pitch content, shape, dynamics and duration. Using chance to determine the events in a composition was a huge step forward for Cage.

Now he began to harness all the elements of his work which had preoccupied him over the last decade in a steady stream of challenging pieces which continued to break new ground: the **Imaginary Landscape No 4** (1951) for twelve radios, each one "played" by two performers who operate independently of each other the volume and tuning controls according to the score; **Williams Mix** (1952) for tape (an early example of musique concrète); and one of his first overtly theatrical pieces; **Water Music** (1952), written "for a pianist, using also a radio, whistles, water containers, a deck of cards, a wooden stick, and objects for preparing a piano." As we have noted, **4'33"** and the Black Mountain event also date from this time.

The theatrical nature of **Water Music** is something which is inherent in all Cage's work involving live performers. Just as he had come to accept that all sound was music, so he regarded all activity, including performing, as theater.

Cage was not the only composer attracted to the idea of using chance, or indeed the only artist. Throughout the course of the 50s it began to appear in the work of several young Americans working in different disciplines, especially in New York. It was not entirely unknown in previous centuries but examples are rare and on the fringe of the mainstream. In 1950s New York it became a definite movement – for Cage, a way of life. Cage had gathered around him a small group of younger composers, Morton Feldman (1926–87), Earle Brown (1926–2003) and Christian Wolff (b.1934), plus the pianist David Tudor (1926–96), who were all interested in exploring new attitudes towards composition and performance.

Their interest was fuelled by the close contact they were developing with other artists. In the case of Cage and Feldman, it was the American Abstract Expressionist painters (Pollock, Rauschenberg etc), with whom they found much in common. Cage's interest in the dance bore fruit in his meeting with the choreographer Merce Cunningham (1919–2009) which began a collaboration lasting for the rest of Cage's life.

The appeal of using chance was that a more random continuity of sounds could be produced and no two performances would be the same. Inevitably this involved devising new methods of notation. In his article "History of Experimental Music in the New States", Cage relates that Wolff made the first steps in this direction. "He wrote some pieces vertically on the page but recommended their being played horizontally left to right, as is conventional".[15] Wolff subsequently developed a highly involved methodology where the production of sounds by each performer would be dependent on a system of cues. Players would be obliged by the notation to play only when permitted by the prevailing conditions, thus preventing any kind of emotional or other involvement and allowing the sounds to happen spontaneously.

Cage observed that, in playing Wolff's music, 'all you can do is suddenly listen in the same way that, when you catch cold, all you can do is suddenly sneeze'.[16] Wolff's notation, a mixture of traditional and newer elements, is surprisingly exact given that the results sound unpredictable. Example 13 is from **For 1, 2 or 3 People** (1964), a characteristically matter-of-fact Wolff title.

Ex.13   Wolff, For 1, 2 or 3 People

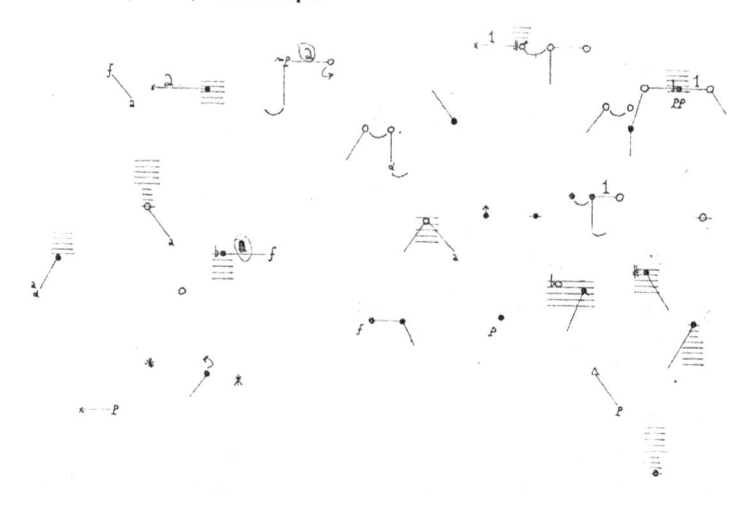

© C.F. Peters Corporation, New York. Reprinted by permission of Peters Edition Limited, London.

Feldman and Brown began to explore other possibilities of graphic notation. Brown produced one of the most radical examples in a piece called simply **December 1952**, which consists of an arrangement of horizontal and vertical straight lines of varying thickness on a single sheet of paper. There are no instructions, Brown transfering all responsibilities for realization firmly with his prospective performers (Example 14).

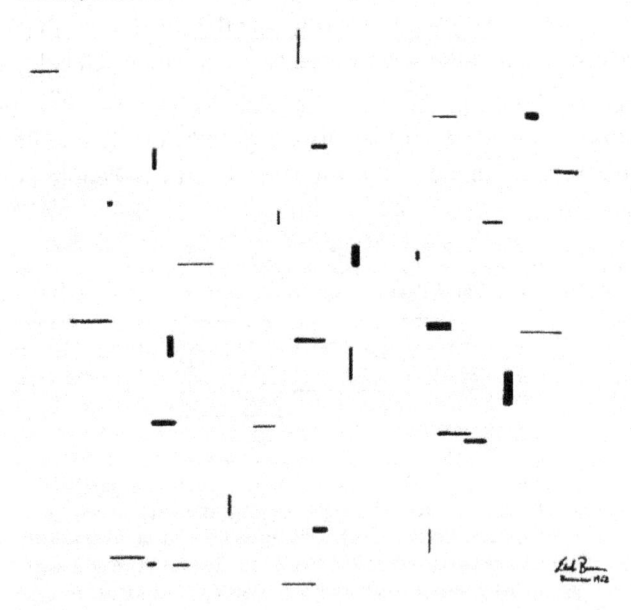

Ex.14   Brown, December 1952 (from *Folio*)

© Copyright 1961 (Renewed) by Associated Music Publishers, Inc. (BMI). All rights reserved. International Copyright secured. Used by permission.

Feldman's early forays into graphic notation can be seen in two groups of pieces, **Projection** (1950–1) and **Intersection** (1951–3). Feldman allows the players to choose their own pitches in the general ranges of high, medium and low, all other parameters (duration, dynamics, etc.) being specified. Example 15 is from **Intersection II** for piano.

Ex.15 Feldman, Intersection II, bars 130–258

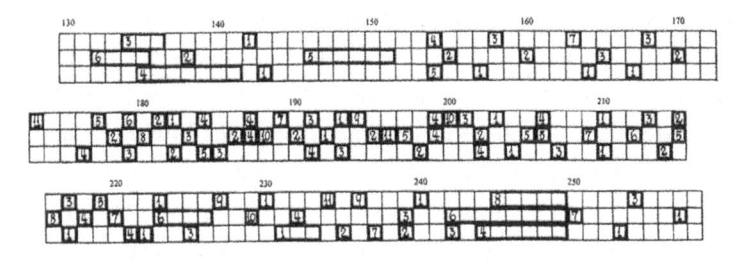

© C.F. Peters Corporation, New York. Reprinted by permission of Peters Edition Limited, London.

In subsequent pieces, Feldman preferred to determine the pitches, and also favored a quiet dynamic level, but left the durations of the sounds free. The effect is of sounds being released into time and space, each one occupying its own portion of the space/time continuum, encouraging the listener to experience the music totally in the present. (In his late works, Feldman forsook all freedoms and used an exact notation.)

Cage was certainly inspired by the notational experiments of Feldman, Brown and Wolff, and was particularly interested in the way a distancing between composer and musical outcome was being created. His increasing involvement with Zen, and the related ideas of, among others, the fourteenth century German mystic Meister Eckhart, had introduced him to the concept of non-intention as a way of achieving the emptiness necessary for self-fulfilment. Cage saw a connection between this and the work he and his colleagues were doing. But using chance to create a fixed result, as he had done in the **Music of Changes**, was no longer the way forward. To achieve non-intention in his work, the sounds in a piece must be allowed to be themselves, free from the intention of the composer. The composition needed to be indeterminate of its performance. He had already achieved this with **4'33"**, an "empty" structure, full of unintended sounds and the purest example of indeterminacy. Cage, however, never one to rest on his laurels, wanted to find other ways to bring about this state of non-intention.

Marking the imperfections in the paper on which he was working gave a random pattern of points and this became a favorite tool along with the random superimposition of differently marked sheets of transparent acetate. Cage puts the onus firmly on the shoulders of the interpreter and it can be a laborious and time-consuming process making a realization of some of these pieces, especially one like **Fontana Mix** (1958) where the materials include sheets of paper containing six varieties of criss-crossing wavy lines, sheets of marked imperfections transferred to acetate, a sheet of graph paper and a straight line, both on acetate.

These are freely superimposed on each other, the resulting combination and its interpretation giving the performers their program of sound events, but they can still choose what sounds to use. Example 16 gives a sample ordering.

Ex.16 Cage, Fontana Mix, sample superimposition of materials

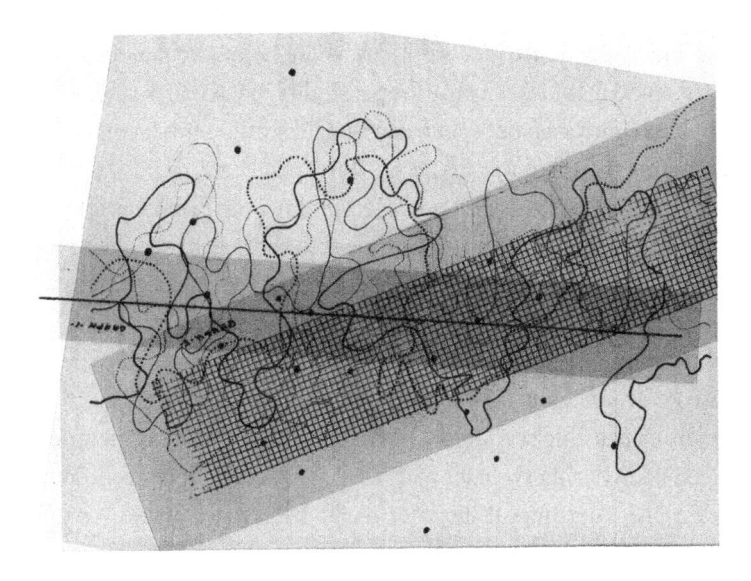

© Henmar Press, Inc., New York. Reprinted by permission of Peters Edition Limited, London.

The spread of Cage's ideas in Europe gathered momentum after his visit to Darmstadt in 1958, where he spoke about his **Music of Changes** and introduced his audience to the concept of indeterminacy. To composers still grappling with the aftermath of integral serialism, this was a difficult concept to accept. There was, not surprisingly, considerable reluctance to try out indeterminacy of pitch, the one parameter still considered sacrosanct, but the area of structure seemed to offer greater, and safer, possibilities.

This became the favored route taken by many European composers, early examples being Boulez's **Third Piano Sonata** (1955–7) and Stockhausen's **Piano Piece XI** (1956). Boulez allows the Sonata's movements to be played in different orders, with certain restrictions, while Stockhausen's piece contains short fragments of music scattered over a large sheet, the pianist being instructed to play them in any sequence, according to where he or she happens to look. This method includes not only the possibility that some fragments might be played more than once, but also that they might not be played at all, an outcome much closer to the spirit of Cage.

The proliferation of open, or mobile, form pieces like these invited some amazingly inventive ideas to surface, as seen for example in **Transición II** (1958–9) by Kagel, a work for pianist, percussionist (who plays the inside of the piano) and two tape recorders. The score features fragments of notation printed on discs and rectangles designed to rotate or slide when attached to other pages, giving the performers numerous possible readings. The first part of the piece is recorded and played back during the later part, while the second tape recorder plays back a pre-recording of the later music before it is heard "live" – an attempt to fuse the past, present and future.

While there are several instances of the use of out-and-out abstract graphic notation, designed to stimulate the interpreter (the phrase is Cornelius Cardew's, in the performance instructions accompanying the score of his **Octet '61**), the sort of controlled indeterminacy described above, for which the favored term is "aleatoricism", is probably more characteristic of the majority of European composers.

Boulez, for one, has remained committed to this procedure. His **Rituel: in memoriam Maderna** (1974–75) divides the symphony orchestra into smaller groups whose material (by turns static and florid) is cued at will by the conductor, giving a complex layering of textures where the vertical alignment of parts *in toto* is of little consequence compared with the overall effect.

Similar techniques can be found in the work of Witold Lutosławski (1913–94). The opening of his **Jeux vénétiens** (1960–1), a piece written as a result of hearing Cage's **Concert for Piano and Orchestra** (1958) though sharing none of that work's almost reckless proliferation of ideas, has the woodwinds of the orchestra playing florid lines on a few selected pitches which together constitute a symmetrical 12-note chord (Example 17). Again, vertical alignment is unimportant and the players can choose their own tempi. The effect is similar to the way Mozart expresses a chord by creating an 'Alberti' figure from its notes. Lutosławski's version is infinitely more complex, of course, but he achieves a comparable harmonic stasis, despite the frenzied activity of the instrumental parts.

Ex.17 Lutosławski, Jeux vénétiens, 12-note chord

Copyright by Mannheimer Musikverlag München

REACTIONS

It is noteworthy that rigorous serialism and indeterminacy/aleatoricism did not appeal to all composers of the 'Darmstadt generation'. Dallapiccola's Italianate love of the singing voice led him to eschew the angularity endemic to integral serialism and to adopt a freer approach to pitch organisation, making it subservient to the expressive demands. A somewhat similar attitude is shown in the work of Berio.

Hans Werner Henze (b.1926) is another member of that generation who soon found himself out of sympathy with what he saw as the narrowness of the ideology. Henze's mind was far too open for that, being attracted as much to Stravinsky as to serialism and inclined towards a general expressivity at odds with the avant-garde who were quick to denounce him as a traitor to the cause, particularly as he was one of the few composers of that period whose work had met with considerable critical and even public acclaim. When Henze left Germany in 1953 and moved to Italy, a country he had previously visited and fallen in love with, it was for personal rather than musical reasons, but the gesture was laden with heavy symbolism (forsaking, as he put it, the 'contrapuntal north for the arioso south').

The move helped to vindicate and encourage his innate sense of lyricism and undogmatic approach to composition, already apparent in such works as his first, highly successful opera, **Boulevard Solitude** (1951) and now flowering confidently in, for example, the **Five Neapolitan Songs** (1956), an even more reactionary work, the engagement with traditional texts tempering any proclivity towards experimentation.[17] It has continued to inform much of his subsequent work, notably in the huge amount of vocal music, including many operas, which now forms a central part of his output.

Henze's identification with Italian life and culture has not resulted in him severing all ties with the country of his birth. He sees himself, and wishes to be seen, as part of the great Germanic tradition. As if to underline the fact, he has remained committed to that supreme monument to German musical achievement, the symphony (more exactly, the sonata principle), which he regards as some sort of ideal. Henze's ten, at this writing, completed symphonies now form almost as much of a central part of his oeuvre as the vocal music; the **First Symphony** dating from 1947, though it was radically revised in 1963, and the **Tenth** finished in 2000.

Of course, as with most other twentieth century composers attracted to symphonic writing, Henze does not have the benefit of the tonal system to bind everything together and so has to rely on other devices, of which rhythmic energy, following the Stravinsky model, is certainly one. This is amply demonstrated in the first movement, called a dance by Henze, of the **Seventh Symphony** (1983–4), though a more distant influence may be the **Seventh Symphony** of Beethoven.

It is, no doubt, the dramatic nature of the sonata principle as much as anything which explains Henze's attraction to the writing of symphonies. The operatic style of Mozart's essays in the genre cannot have gone unnoticed but, in any case, extra-musical influences are evident in the vast majority of Henze's instrumental music which, as with Birtwistle, tends towards the condition of theater. An especially potent example is **Tristan** (1973), a huge, 45-minute work for piano, electronic tape and orchestra.

The circumstances surrounding the work's genesis and ultimate realization relate to a series of traumatic personal experiences which seem to be responsible for its more radical nature. The opening piano solo sets the scene for what follows. Its abstract and disjunct textures hark back to the 50s avant-garde style which Henze had rebelled against but the violent expressionism of the ensuing pages of the score, especially the taped insertions and quotations, often distorted, of other music, is quite unprecedented in Henze's work. The quotation from the opening of Act 3 of Wagner's **Tristan und Isolde** is related to the nightmares about the figure of Tristan which Henze apparently experienced before embarking on the piece and which subsequently suggested its content.[18]

EXPERIMENTALISM

The example of Cage ushered in one of the most fertile periods in the twentieth century, one in which experimentation and iconoclasm were rife and frontiers between different artistic disciplines became blurred. Younger composers seized eagerly on his innovations in both the fearless exploration and exploitation of sound and the theatrical aspects of performance. If there were occasions when composers and performers became the victims of self-indulgence and irresponsibility (as when the Korean artist Nam June Paik (1932–2006), during a concert, took a pair of scissors and cut off the end of John Cage's tie), this was more than compensated for by the sheer variety of truly imaginative pieces from composers such as Alvin Lucier (b.1931), with his scientific investigations into the acoustic properties of different environments and their effects on the behaviour of sound.

The image, in his **Music for Solo Performer** (1964–5) of the performer, his skull wired up to a high-amplification system, surrounded by loudspeakers and an assortment of percussion instruments, sitting motionless and allowing his brain to produce a steady stream of alpha rhythms which are heard through the speakers and in turn excite the percussion by sympathetic vibration, is one not readily forgotten.

Groups

This period also saw the emergence of several small ensembles, all featuring electronics to some degree, through which experimental composers might propagate their work. One such, the Sonic Arts Group (later the Sonic Arts Union), was founded by Lucier with the composers David Behrman (b.1937), Gordon Mumma (b.1935) and Robert Ashley (b.1930). Others appeared in Europe, notably Musica Elettronica Viva (MEV), based in Rome though consisting largely of Americans, including the redoubtable pianist/composer Frederic Rzewski (b.1938), and Stockhausen's group, for whom he wrote many graphic scores, for example **Prozession** (1967) and **Plus-Minus** (1963) and also text scores like the collection **Aus den sieben Tagen** (1968), all intended for improvisation, albeit controlled by Stockhausen himself, never one to allow others too much limelight. (Much of MEV's work centered round free improvisation.)

English Experimental Music

There was a particularly lively scene in England with groups like AMM, Intermodulation and Gentle Fire. AMM, whose founder members were jazz musicians who had become disillusioned with what they perceived as the restrictions in jazz, dedicated themselves solely to free improvisation and are still active. Improvisation was also central to the work of Gentle Fire, though they preferred the term Group Composition, and both they and Intermodulation played pieces by their members and other established experimental composers.

An important part of the English scene was the pioneering work of Cornelius Cardew (1936–81) who had been an assistant to Stockhausen in the early 60s but subsequently aligned himself more with Cage. (He also became a regular member of AMM.) Cardew was interested in the demarcation between amateur and professional, aware that much experimental music lay within reach of the former (or even the non-musician), and believed that the division might be breached through collective improvisation, the composer acting as facilitator. Thus came into being works like the **Octet '61**, the monumental, 193-page, graphic score **Treatise** (1963–7), and **The Great Learning** (1968–70), with texts by Confucius.

It was while working on this latter piece that Cardew formed the notorious Scratch Orchestra, a motley collection of musicians and other artists of every hue, plus assorted hangers-on. Cardew was able to realize his ideas with the Orchestra though these, with the changing sociopolitical situation through the war in Vietnam and the fading of the 60s' dream of "freedom", began to take on a more aggressively political front, going so far as to identify the struggle against corporate domination in the arts with that of the revolutionary movements in Ireland and China.

Cardew suddenly performed an extraordinary volte-face, rejecting all experimentation in favor of a more overtly popular style – basically protest songs with simple melodies and guitar-friendly chord sequences. His example was followed by Christian Wolff and Rzewski, by then close colleagues, the three of them effectively turning their backs on the avant-garde they had helped to create.

It is interesting to compare the attitude of Cardew and his circle towards social and political commitment with that shown by, for example Nono, Henze, Britten or Tippett; all left-of-centre composers who have nevertheless preferred not to compromise their musical language in the expression of their indignation. Nono's use of "found" sounds, for instance the recorded street demonstrations in **Contrappunto dialettico alla mente** (1967–8) and Britten's juxtaposition of war poetry with the Latin text of the Mass for the Dead in the **War Requiem** (1962) both in their different ways seek to communicate to the ordinary listener potent images of inequality, injustice and outrage, through music which also uplifts the spirit.

Not all of Cardew's circle followed his political course, however much they may have been in sympathy with him, and his change of direction was widely greeted with incomprehension, even dismay. Howard Skempton (b.1947), once a close associate, has since pursued a totally independent path. Skempton's preference for quiet dynamic levels and a leisurely pace show the influence of Feldman but his self-effacing, disarmingly simple style, with its frequent touches of gentle humor, owes more to Satie and seems to occupy a private world into which the listener enters almost apologetically. These characteristics were fairly typical of English experimental music of the time, including many of the Scratch Orchestra's projects, though there was also a tendency towards plain silliness, due mostly to a misunderstanding of the messages that Cage and others had been putting out.

The career of the notorious Portsmouth Sinfonia was regarded in this light by many people who could simply not take seriously the idea that there was any value to be had in listening to a group of (mostly) unskilled, though enthusiastic, amateurs giving renditions of popular classics by playing whatever they could remember of the scores – such being the Sinfonia's brief.

The fact that the players were nearly all art students did not help. (Art colleges, rather than music colleges, proved a receptive environment for experimental music at this period.) But the Sinfonia, which numbered among its ranks such names as Brian Eno (b.1948) and Gavin Bryars (b.1943), was serious, in an English experimental sort of way, and their performances had a heroic quality which could be strangely moving.

Bryars's own music of this period has a similarly ironic, slightly tongue-in-cheek quirkiness, as in, for example, **The Squirrel and the Ricketty-Racketty Bridge** (1971), for one or more electric guitars laid on their backs, the player(s) performing a series of ascending patterns in a regular rhythm by "walking" their fingers up the fingerboard creating an audio-visual picture of the old children's tale.

Bryars has retained his ironic persona but he has developed an idiom which occupies a position independent of most of the prevailing limbs of contemporary compositional practice. This has largely come about through a deep interest in and predilection for what he has identified as an "alternative" branch of early modernism, which includes such eccentric figures as Satie, Busoni, Percy Grainger (1882–1961) and Lord Berners (1883–1950) and also, intriguingly, Rachmaninov.[19]

Bryars has also never lost his fondness for chromatic harmony, a legacy partly of his early career as a jazz double-bassist but also of what one may detect as a streak of sentimentality. The Hymns Ancient and Modern-style harmonies with which Bryars cloaks the voice of his recorded tramp in his justly celebrated **Jesus' Blood Never Failed me Yet** (1971–4) was a sure indication of the direction Bryars was moving in.

From the 1980s, all these influences coalesced into a style featuring wisps of lyrical melody, often mildly allusive, set against ambiguous chord progressions gently pulsing or arpeggiating at an unhurried tempo. It is a simple enough style, superficially reminiscent of Michael Nyman (b.1944) and Philip Glass (b.1937), though Bryars avoids the unfortunate banality to which they are prone.

The Spirit of Independence Continued

The dominant figure of Cage is a reminder of the independence frequently shown by American composers, a trait which goes back to Ives and Cowell. Cowell's championing of primitive and non-western music was of supreme importance to Lou Harrison (1917–2003) and Harry Partch (1901–74), who were among several Americans who regarded the European tradition since the Renaissance as an aberration, deflecting music from its true nature. The development of equal temperament, an artificial conception when all is said and done, and the concomitant rise of functional harmony, were the real bones of contention and both Harrison and Partch sought to return to more "natural" systems.

Partch settled on a system of 43 tones to the octave, basically a just intonation with microtonal extensions, which necessitated the building of new instruments, or adaptation of existing ones, an activity which occupied Partch for some 40-odd years. Harrison, however, never used any system exclusively though he was particularly influenced by that found in the Indonesian gamelan where each gamelan is tuned in a specific way so that it and its music form a unique entity.

Harrison was, in fact, influenced by a wide variety of non-western, and pre-Renaissance, music and saw no problem in combining them in the same piece. He was even, interestingly, and slightly perversely, happy to put up with instruments tuned in equal temperament, believing that hybridization through "acculturation"(his term) is the best means of survival.

The music of both Harrison and Partch is almost exclusively centered on melody, rhythm and timbre. Harmony, where it exists, has no function other than a vaguely decorative or coloristic one. Harrison's penchant for oriental musics can be observed in his melodic style and frequent use of ostinato. He also, like his friend John Cage, took a special delight in what is generally called "junk percussion" though Harrison's use of it was more conventional than Cage's. Harrison was envious of Cage's invention of the prepared piano ("Damn; I wish I'd thought of that") but would never have considered using a radio, as Cage had done. Among the novelties in Harrison's work may be cited the eight rice bowls tuned to an exotic 'gapped' scale and the set of six different sized baker's pans, yielding an approximate 'scale', in the **Varied Trio** (1986) for violin, piano and percussion.

Partch was an altogether different animal. Much of his inspiration came from the life and social customs of ordinary American people, treated as though they were contemporary myths. Thus a group of graffiti provided the impetus for the short work **Barstow – Eight Hitchhiker Inscriptions from a Highway Railing at Barstow, California** (1941, rev. 1968). The texts, which express uninhibitedly the thoughts, feelings and frustrations of people waiting for a lift, are set to a curious mixture of simple folk-style singing and heightened speech, the latter often humorous in the way it swoops and slides.

It is a style of vocal performance closely related to blues singing and other vernacular idioms, though it also retains a uniqueness thanks to the way it has to adapt to the amazing sounds coming from the accompanying instruments.

Partch's instruments, with their fanciful names and often stunning physical appearance (considered by Partch to be as important as their sound) are by anyone's reckoning one of the twentieth century's most impressive monuments to man's inventiveness.

Many of them are based on existing instruments, extended or adapted to fit Partch's tuning system but in some cases acquiring unconventional shapes (which then demand a special notation). Thus the Adapted Guitar, Adapted Viola, Surrogate Kithara and Diamond Marimba. Others make use of "found objects" or junk. This group contains the delicate and almost irreplaceable Cloud Chamber Bowls (large upturned glass bowls used in studying atomic particles), Mazda Marimba (tuned light bulbs) and the Bloboy (a large bellows connected to a set of car horns and organ pipes).

The building of new instruments, both acoustic and electronic, is a not uncommon activity among experimental composers based on the Pacific coast of America and Partch, a Californian, was one of the most highly regarded of a generally resourceful collection of individuals. His instruments are so bound up with the music he wrote that one can, with justification, refer to them as his personal gamelan. As with the gamelan, it is possible to write new works for them, and this has in fact been done by some of Partch's acolytes, but one cannot use them to perform any existing repertoire.

Nancarrow

Independence of a different kind is seen in the extraordinary figure of Conlon Nancarrow, born in 1912 but hardly known before the 1980s. Nancarrow envisioned a music of such complexity as to put it beyond the capabilities of human performers. Unsurprisingly, given Nancarrow's background in jazz, this complexity lay in the field of rhythm, usually featuring his favored device of highly intricate canonic structures which create dense polyphonic textures whose several layers maintain differing degrees of independence from each other.

THE MUSIC OF
CONLON NANCARROW
Kyle Gann

To solve the problem of performance, Nancarrow turned to an instrument which seemed eminently practical and foolproof; the player piano, or pianola. Its technology of paper rolls punched with holes corresponding to the notes of the music, which the piano plays automatically, was an early form of recording, but Nancarrow quickly saw that he could produce exactly the complex rhythmic schemes he envisaged by punching the holes in the paper himself on his own machine.

Thus, from the late 1940s on, Nancarrow, in complete isolation from the rest of the musical world, began his series of **Studies** for pianola, a large and impressive body of work which constitutes the greater part of his catalog. The inventiveness manifested in these pieces is truly staggering: some are inspired by boogie-woogie and piano blues, the rolling rhythms made more lopsided by Nancarrow's rhythmic schemes; others are more abstract, revelling in their own rhythmic conceits.

Nancarrow's canonic procedures are far removed from the standard model where the second voice shadows the first exactly and at an easily perceived distance such as a couple of beats, a bar or short phrase, as in the familiar rounds *'London's Burning'* or *'Frère Jacques'*. Nancarrow's canons usually involve such devices as simultaneous different meters and/or tempi where the distance between the voices can be expressed as a ratio.

One of the simplest examples is **Study No.14**, where the two simultaneous tempi are quarter note = 110 and quarter note = 88; a ratio of 4:5.[20] Other studies employ much more complex relationships, sometimes involving irrational values. Furthermore, a canonic voice is not necessarily a single-note melodic line but may be, and frequently is, a succession of different sound-events: chords, glissandi, trills etc.

The ability to punch one's rhythmic ideas onto a paper roll means that pretty much anything is possible. So Nancarrow makes use of chordal glissandi, repeated notes and all manner of abstract figurations at impossibly fast speeds, as well as the superhuman rhythms, all of which combine and flash past the ear of the bemused listener who also knows that they are hearing a piano do things it was never intended to do. The humor in this, as well as the intricacy of detail, has not been lost on György Ligeti (1923–2006), much of whose work exhibits similar qualities. His own **Etudes** for piano, a series begun in 1985, though obviously not of the same order of complexity, being written for human performers, nevertheless hover dangerously close to the limits of human virtuosity.

Texture

Ligeti is one of a group of Eastern European composers who quickly rose to prominence during the 1960s, due to the novel and, at the time, provocative emphasis on texture and timbre at the expense of other considerations in their work. This was something which had attracted the imagination of Debussy earlier in the century but it was the development of electronic music which inspired these Eastern Europeans to explore the possibilities of constructing entire works on textural and timbral bases. Ligeti was particularly fortunate in that, having fled to Germany in the wake of the Hungarian uprising in 1956, he had found refuge with Stockhausen at the time of the latter's early experiments with the new technology and become fascinated by what was being achieved.

Ligeti's own work in the WDR studio remained exploratory but the contact with tape technology paid off in the instrumental and vocal works which were to follow. His orchestral piece **Lontano** (1967) takes the listener on an unpredictable journey as the initial solitary Ab gradually grows into a series of ever-changing clouds of sound, as notes and instrumental colors come and go, the whole process dictated solely by the composer's ear. The instruments are largely confined to playing long-held notes but individual details are obscured by the overall effect, clearly showing the influence of electronic music. The static nature of Ligeti's works at this time was something that could not be upheld for long if a certain sameness were to be avoided. Writing a piece for solo harpsichord presented an obvious problem in this respect. The instrument's inability to sustain sound meant seeking an alternative and in **Continuum** (1968), written for the harpsichordist Antoinette Vischer, Ligeti makes use of rapid repeated notes while still maintaining a slow rate of harmonic and textural change.

But the most far-reaching development came later with the composer's gradual introduction of what he termed 'micro-polyphony', where the sustained notes are replaced by lines which typically move by small chromatic steps in such a way as to make them difficult to distinguish (a technique adumbrated by Bartók in the first movement of his **Music for String Instruments, Percussion and Celesta**). This became, for Ligeti, a means of achieving some fantastic flights of aural imagination where tiny, intricate figures combine to produce textures of almost otherworldly proportions. Early instances of the technique appear in the **Second String Quartet** (1968) and the **Chamber Concerto** (1969–70), continuing and developing further with the orchestral **Melodien** (1971) – the lines more obviously 'melodic' here – and entering the realm of surrealism with the opera **Le Grand Macabre** (1974–8). There is a feverish excitement to these scores and it comes as no surprise to learn of Ligeti's fascination with mechanical toys and other devices, his interest in artists like Paul Klee and his deep respect for the unbounded imaginative world of childhood. Hence also his attraction to the work of Nancarrow as well as to certain aspects of minimalism.

Another important figure is Krzysztof Penderecki (b.1933), whose celebrated **Threnody for the Victims of Hiroshima (Tren)** for 52 solo strings (1959–61) approaches even closer to the sound-world of electronic music through the use of quarter-tone clusters. When these are made to glissando, the effect is even more striking. Example 18 shows Penderecki's method of notation.

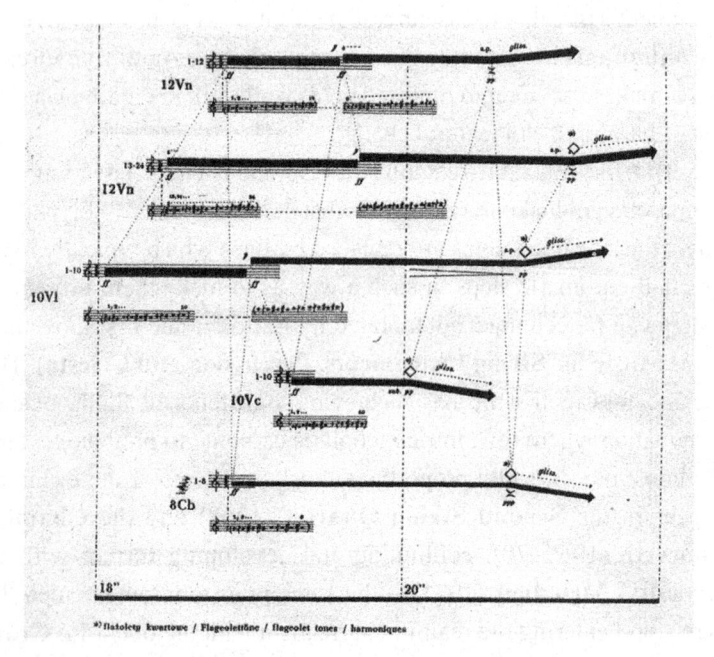

Ex.18   Penderecki, Tren. p.8

© 1975 Deshon Music Inc. EMI United Partnership Ltd, London, WC2 (Publishing) and Alfred Publishing Co, USA (Print). Administered in Europe by Faber Music Ltd. All rights reserved.

A further aspect of this music is the discovery of new and unusual sounds and playing techniques. String players might be asked to play behind the bridge, or to strike the body of the instrument, for example, and wind players to produce chords (a technique known as multiphonics). The central section of **Tren** is a compendium of such "extended techniques" for the strings.

2
MINIMALISM

THE ORIGINS OF MINIMALISM CAN be traced back to the late 1950s when American experimental music was reaching maturity. John Cage's emancipation of the single sound encouraged other composers to devise pieces which concentrated on singularities for their own sake: for example, a sound, a performance gesture, an action. The artists of the Fluxus movement produced some of the most celebrated examples, like George Brecht's (b.1924) **Piano Piece 1962 – "A vase of flowers on(to) a piano."** (This is the title of the piece *and* the score).

There is a clear indebtedness here not only to Cage and Zen but also to Duchamp and Dada and the composition of such pieces was not solely the province of composers. The later establishment in London by Cornelius Cardew of the Scratch Orchestra, a project owing much to the example of Fluxus, was a sort of manifestation that anyone could be a composer i.e. could devise a composition, just as his **Octet '61** postulated that anyone could be a performer i.e. could interpret a score.

Central to this activity in America was La Monte Young (b.1935), whose early work showed a similar fascination for singularities but with an added dimension: the sustaining of the singularity for a long period of time, a characteristic that originates in Young's childhood experiences of listening to the humming of telephone wires in the Idaho outback.

Young noticed the way the sound changed as he shifted his position in relation to it, or when the wind affected it, and the recognition that by sustaining a sound one becomes aware of its inner life is crucial to Young's work. Thus the drone became, and has remained, his chief preoccupation, apparent in the early **Composition 1960 #7**, which calls for the perfect fifth B-F# 'to be held for a long time', the **Drift Study** (1973) for electronic oscillators and the various components of the **Dream House**, the more or less continuous sound environment in which he lives.

Young has always favored complex drones, typically the perfect intervals in just intonation, hence his preference for electronic oscillators, which can keep their pitch almost indefinitely. The drones may be either left by themselves and listened to in quiet contemplation of their beauty, or used as a basis for improvisation, the players working closely with the given pitches and contributing to the basic sound, rather than indulging in 'personal expression'.

Young also developed an expertise in tuning the humble grand piano in just intonation, a skill which led to the composition (begun in 1964 and still apparently unfinished) of **The Well-Tuned Piano**, essentially a controlled improvisation on groups of chords and lasting upwards of five hours. The improvisations, at least as played by the composer, are in the nature of decorative patterns, permutating a series of pitches, and thus make for a much busier experience than the static drone pieces, though the busyness is somewhat an illusion.

Interestingly, at the time of the emergence of Young's series of **Compositions 1960**, modern jazz, in which Young had been heavily involved, was entering a phase where the improvisation was based on a largely unchanging modal structure rather than functional harmony, underpinned by, if not actual drones, either ostinati or some constant reference to a modal final. Real drones and repetition are also, of course, features of much non-western music and Young was quickly drawn towards such musical cultures, particularly Indian and Tibetan, as was his friend and exact contemporary Terry Riley (b.1935), both of whom have studied Indian singing with Pandit Pran Nath. Both Young and Riley are therefore important links in the continuing crossing-over of western art music, jazz and oriental music.

1960s electronic technology, increasingly ubiquitous on the experimental music scene, might have been expected to have played an important role here, since drones and repetitive patterns are easy to produce on analog synthezisers, but the rather ugly nature of the sounds never proved attractive to the minimalists. Instead, the same effects were achieved by tape loops.[21] This was the favored method of Terry Riley and another important pioneer, Steve Reich (b.1936).

It was, however, an instrumental piece that really kickstarted the whole minimalist movement, though the word had not yet been applied. This was Terry Riley's **In C** (1964). Fifty-three fragments of music are repeated, in sequence, any number of times by any number of players using any appropriate instruments or voices, in a live version of tape loop technique. The repetitiveness, slow rate of change as the piece progresses and the natural phasing which occurred as individual performers moved out of synch with each other, created a trance-like situation, made all the more potent by the unblemished (save for 2 chromatic intrusions) C major tonality[22] and the fast pulse which held everything together.

In one fell swoop, Riley had united the worlds of experimental music, modal jazz and oriental music, sowing considerable confusion among the ranks of the "purist" avant-garde and, perhaps unwittingly, changing the face of contemporary music for ever. Riley has remained faithful to improvisation (implicit in **In C**), exploiting the connections with jazz and Indian music and usually employing just intonation, and it was left to Reich and his close contemporary Philip Glass (b.1937) to develop the motivic aspects of Riley's work.

From the late 1960s, Reich and Glass produced a stream of work in which the essential elements of repetition, modality and pulse were deployed in a variety of settings. Reich's experiments with tape loops led to his discovery of phasing, as happened when two identical loops were played simultaneously on two tape recorders. An inherent "fault" of analog tape recorders causes one machine to run slightly ahead of the other, creating a shimmering effect which keeps changing as the two loops move further apart.

If multiplied several times over, the effect can be stunning, and Reich duly took advantage of this to create two pieces: **It's Gonna Rain** (1965) and **Come Out** (1966). In both pieces, the sounds on the loops are samples of recorded speech. It is surprising how melodic speech can be, but the sing-song quality of the voices in these two pieces, a black preacher and black youth respectively, as well as their strong rhythmic profile, results in a kind of primitive, modal chant. The effect of the multiple phasing process on the phonemes of the phrases creates a complex texture of drones and percussion which eventually reaches a point where the text becomes indecipherable, every phoneme being heard simultaneously.

Steve Reich (right) with the author at a workshop at Leeds College of Music, England

One curious by-product of working with this technology was that the gradual and inexorable process of transformation of the material was, in a sense, outside the composer's control; once the machines were set up, the piece more or less wrote itself and the composer could simply sit back and listen and accept the consequences.

Composition and performance were fused. For this reason, Reich coined the term "process music" to describe the new methodology ("minimalism" came into use later). Reich soon learned to apply the technique of phasing to live performance and his next pieces attempted to put this into practice. One of these is **Piano Phase** (1967) for two pianos. The piece starts with the two pianists playing the basic pattern, a modal figure of twelve even sixteenth notes in unison. The phasing effect is achieved by having one player accelerate their part slightly until they are one semiquaver ahead of their partner, then accelerating again until they are two sixteenth notes ahead, and so on until the two pianists arrive back at unison – and thus ends the first section. The overall effect is still somewhat similar to **Come Out** but, as Reich quickly realized, the technique has lots of potential for further elaboration.

One important development, another by-product of the phasing process, was the creation of what Reich calls 'resulting patterns'. When a pattern is played out of phase with itself, the ear will detect other melodic and/or rhythmic patterns which are the result of the special relationship at that moment between the two parts i.e. the way they interlock. This phenomenon is familiar to anyone who has experienced the complex polyphonic structures in some traditional African music.

Reich's discovery of it in his own music was a contributing factor in his decision to study African drumming at its source and he spent a few weeks in Ghana in 1970 in the company of a master drummer of the Ewe tribe. He also made detailed studies of Balinese gamelan music, which has certain affinities with African drum music, especially in the matter of the interlocking of small rhythmic motifs. Reich's direction was now pretty clear and over the next couple of decades his music became increasingly more sophisticated in the deployment of the techniques he had learned. His pieces are for varying groups of players with percussion always at the center.

These pieces range from the simple and self-explanatory **Clapping Music** (1972) for two performers to the huge four-movement **Drumming** (1970–1) for assorted percussion, including female voices, whistling and piccolo. Reich's predilection for the hard-edged sonorities of percussion, keyboards, woodwind and voices obliged him to form his own, essentially acoustic, ensemble, Steve Reich and Musicians, which has remained his favored performing outlet to this date.

While Reich was developing his technical armory, Philip Glass was struggling to find his own direction, which did not crystallize until the mid 60s when he met and began working with the renowned sitar player Ravi Shankar (b.1920). Through Shankar, and his usual tabla player Allah Rakha (1919–2000), Glass entered into the colorful and exciting world of Indian classical music, in those days still something of a novelty, and immediately became interested in the rhythmic techniques employed, principally the concept that rhythm is created by adding different durations together; the exact opposite of the Western concept of parcelling up a length of time into neat groupings of three or four beats.

Of course, this was the same concept that had influenced Messiaen several years previously though it is not certain that Glass was aware of this. In any case, Glass had made his discovery independently of the older composer and in the best possible manner – at the feet of two masters of the art.

The discovery of Indian classical music helped to set Glass on his way and his next pieces show him experimenting with Indian additive technique on extremely simple materials, clearly still feeling his way. **Strung Out** for solo violin (1967) is based on a simple five-note motif: a rising minor third E-G followed by a descending scale fragment E-D-C in the octave above, played as even eighth notes. Glass modifies the technique to one of expansion and contraction of the motif, but not in any systematic way. The method is rather one of continuous variation, almost like an improvisation, the incessant quaver movement giving the ear no clues as to where the music is heading.

Glass's intuitive approach contrasts vividly with the inexorable logic of Reich's early phase pieces, suggesting that Glass wanted to distance himself as much as possible from his colleague's achievements, especially as they both obviously felt they were onto something new. Nevertheless, a greater degree of rigor began to creep into Glass's music, as can be seen in the functionally titled **Music in Fifths** (1969) whose expansion/contraction technique is more carefully controlled. The monotony of the sound of unchanging parallel fifths (no instrumentation is specified) worked against the success of the piece but, although Glass was more adventurous in this respect in later pieces, he remained, and has remained, remarkably faithful to the use of simple materials; basically scale and arpeggio fragments.

The strong relationship with oriental music that minimalism had during this time (what we might call its classic period) was especially apparent in the way it was experienced by the listener. Instead of themes, drama, recapitulation of material, teleological harmony and the other trappings of Western classical music, minimalism's sound-world was static and contemplative, a slow, gradually unfolding process, experienced totally in the present. During the 1970s, however, both Glass and Reich began to incorporate more harmonic change into their music, perhaps sensing that no further development along previous lines was possible or desirable. A key moment for Glass was his meeting with the American artist/producer Robert Wilson (b.1941) which led to the creation of the first of several compositions for the stage; the opera **Einstein on the Beach** (1975). The work is more a series of tableaux than an opera in the usual sense of the term, but Glass was obliged to be more adventurous harmonically though interestingly the other elements of his style remained unchanged.

An important motif in **Einstein on the Beach** is the chord progression, Fm, Db, A, B, E, in simple triads. In the section called Spaceship (Act IV Scene 3), this is repeated round and round for nearly three-quarters of the 13½ minutes duration, varied largely by expansion and contraction of the durations of the chords, the accompanying patterns changing accordingly.

Glass has continued to show a marked preference for such triadic harmony, only rarely stretching it to include mild dissonances, and it is one of the factors which have led to his courtship by the popular music fraternity, reminding us of the close ties that have always existed between the two worlds.

Glass, in turn, has demonstrated his affection for popular music in two grandly conceived orchestral works, the **"Low" Symphony** (1992) and the **"Heroes" Symphony** (1996), respectively his first and fourth symphonies, and both based on albums by David Bowie and Brian Eno from the 1970s. Neither work is particularly symphonic in the accepted sense of the term, Glass avoiding any sense of thematic development, but the latter was taken up by the American choreographer Twyla Tharp and used for a ballet by her company.

Much of Glass's success has been with artists of other disciplines, especially ballet and dance, but also film and, as we have noted, the stage. One of his greatest achievements was the score for Godfrey Reggio's film **Koyaanisqatsi** (1982) where his trademark scalic/arpeggiated patternings fitted perfectly with both the speeded-up shots of urban congestion and the slowed-down images of the natural world.

Glass's relatively simple harmonic language contrasts vividly with that of Reich, who favors the richer sound of modally-derived eleventh and other 'suspended' chords which, paradoxically, help to retain the floating feeling of classic minimalism. This is certainly the case with early 70s works such as **Music for Mallet Instruments, Voices and Organ** (1973), where the rate of harmonic change (the harmonic rhythm) is very slow, but the same feeling is present in later works where the harmonic rhythm is quicker, for instance in **Electric Counterpoint** (1987), written for the jazz guitarist Pat Metheny (b.1954), which, though unmistakably Reichian, also acknowledges the kind of jazz in which Metheny is involved (Example 19).

Ex.19 Reich, Electric Counterpoint, Chord progression, measures 1–8

© Copyright 1989 by Hendon Music Inc. Reproduced by kind permission of Boosey & Hawkes Music Publishers Ltd.

In recent times, Reich has begun collaborating with his wife, the video artist Beryl Korot, in a series of "video operas" on subjects drawn from current affairs. The style is still recognizably Reichian but the composer has added an extra ingredient, one which has its origin in the tape pieces of the 60s and which resurfaced in **Different Trains** (1988), for string quartet and tape; namely, the use of speech patterns as motivic material, a technique also once associated with Janáček. In this piece, phrases spoken by people telling of their experiences on the train journey across America during the Second World War are heard on tape, woven into the fabric of the piece, the pitches and rhythms imitated exactly by the quartet. (Also on the tape are parts for three extra string quartets.)

This technique was developed by Reich in the first of his collaborations with Korot, the ambitious **The Cave** (1993), where various individuals appear on the video screens reciting texts concerning the supposedly common origins of Christianity, Judaism and Islam in the cave at Hebron. In the later **City Life** (1995), for amplified ensemble, Reich made similar use of samples of the sounds of everyday life in his native New York City – car horns, piledrivers, doorslams, etc.

3
POST-MINIMALISM

ADAMS, TORKE, BANG ON A CAN

THE NEW DEVELOPMENTS FROM THE 1970s on, discussed above, marked the beginning of the end for classic minimalism. With the casting off of static modality in favor of more dynamic harmonic schemes, the oriental quality, perhaps minimalism's most distinguishing characteristic, was lost, and the music entered a more familiar world, akin to jazz and popular music, and even in some cases, earlier twentieth century modernism. This is certainly the impression one receives when listening to the music of another American, John Adams.

A decade younger than the four pioneers already discussed, Adams (b.1947) gained his reputation early with works like **Harmonium** (1981) and **Grand Pianola Music** (1982) where harmonies, articulated by energetic repetitive figures, and underpinned by the ubiquitous pulse, are made to change very slowly, giving the impression, as Adams himself likes to suggest, of flying low over a changing landscape. In later works like the **Violin Concerto** (1993) or **Chamber Symphony** (1992), the surface texture, patterning, and even the harmonic scheme are much more complex, with only the pulse reminding us of the composer's minimalist roots, though that too is inevitably not always noticeable.

If Adams is moving further away from minimalism towards a more eclectic modernism, there are plenty of younger American composers for whom it is still an important source of inspiration. It has, in fact, become part of the reservoir of available twentieth century idioms, which now include pop music, especially its newer vernaculars such as techno, hip-hop, house and ambient, as well as jazz and rock. Minimalism's family likeness with these idioms gives it a particular relevance to post-minimalist composers and they have not been slow in turning this to their advantage, but the simple fusion of repetitive structures with gestures derived from pop music or jazz may only produce bland results.

Michael Torke's (b.1961) **The Yellow Pages** (1985) and **Adjustable Wrench** (1987) suffer from a lack of imagination in the treatment of the models (respectively, pop music and big band jazz), whereas a similar fusion plus the added zest of complex, sometimes irrational, rhythms and dissonant harmony in the work of Michael Gordon (b.1956), offers a more compelling mixture, the different ingredients grinding and reverberating against each other in a constantly engaging dialogue.

It is, in fact, interesting to note that dissonance and atonality have re-entered the arena from which they had formerly been banished at the time of minimalism's emergence. Nevertheless, Gordon's harmonies, whatever their degree of dissonance, remain constant for appreciable lengths of time, in the best minimalist tradition, enough to create a feeling of a tonal or modal center. The technique is seen at its best in a work like **Trance** (1995), where the ensemble is divided into several smaller units, each with its own repetitive rhythmic scheme, creating complex, powerful textures of immense energy (Example 20.)

Ex.20   Gordon, Trance, measures 532-535

© Copyright 1992 by Red Poppy (ASCAP). All rights administered by G. Schirmer Inc. (ASCAP). All rights reserved. International Copyright secured. Used by permission.

Gordon is one of the founders, along with David Lang (b.1957) and Julia Wolfe (b.1958), of the Bang on a Can Festival, held annually in New York. These three, now known collectively as The Red Poppies, after the name of their own publishing group, are therefore in a position of considerable influence, for the festival features not only their own work but also that of many like-minded young composers, mostly but not all American; composers who are equally at home in classical as well as jazz, rock or pop music and are not afraid to combine elements of them all together.

This is the new, experimental wing of the American avant-garde: loud, abrasive, aggressive, eccentric and, surprisingly, often virtuosic. The festival's house band, The Bang on a Can All-Stars, a virtuosic band if ever there was one, give authentic and committed performances, thus encouraging composers to stretch further the possibilities of crossover. They have also, in the interests of balance, made an arrangement of one of the signature works of soft-centered ambient music, **Music for Airports** (1979) by the English composer and record producer Brian Eno.

TOTALISM

Gordon is often linked with the so-called totalist composers, including Rhys Chatham (b.1952) and Glenn Branca (b.1949), whose work is similarly characterized by thick textures of piled-up rhythms, articulated in their case by ensembles of massed electric guitars playing at full volume and, in Branca's work at least, in microtonal tunings. The frequent addition of a rock drummer locates his music particularly on the thin divide between minimalism and rock and indeed his grandly titled Symphonies often sound like abstract rock.

ANDRIESSEN AND MARTLAND

Related to American post-minimalism is the work of the iconoclastic English composer Steve Martland (b.1959) and his one-time teacher, the Dutchman Louis Andriessen (b.1939). Being only slightly younger than the first generation American minimalists, Andriessen developed his particular brand of the idiom alongside theirs and though there are superficial similarities, his work is noticeably different in its harmonic style, which derives largely from Stravinsky but with a greater degree of dissonance.

The Russian master is also, inevitably, a source for Andriessen's rhythmic elasticity, but equally strong is the influence of jazz and medieval hocket technique.[23] The listener will find ample evidence of these concerns working their passage through some of Andriessen's scores of the 1970s; the aptly named **Hoketus** (1975–77), for example, an exhilarating duel between two identical amplified groups of keyboards, panpipes, congas and bass guitars (+ optional saxophones), or the ambitious **De staat** (1973–76) for a larger ensemble, an early instance of Andriessen's increasing propensity towards works of social or political intent, conceived on a grand scale.

Several aspects of Andriessen's style are echoed in the music of Steve Martland, the political angle being particularly strong and a source of antagonism to many observers. Indeed, his outspoken frustration at the injustices of the education and cultural situations in post-Thatcher Britain have arguably punctured his progress as a composer. Certainly, the promise of the works of his early maturity, like the exciting, Dutch-inspired **Shoulder to Shoulder** (1986) and **American Invention** (1985) has hardly been realized, subsequent pieces traversing pretty much the same ground.

Pärt and Others

In 1976 the Estonian composer Arvo Pärt (b.1935) emerged from a seven-year period of withdrawal and reassessment with a sequence of works which were to shift yet again the center of gravity of contemporary music, already polarized by the incursion of minimalism into high modernism.

Beginning with **Für Aline**, a simple piano piece, Pärt offered an altogether unique and completely unexpected new style which, with its unsullied modality and air of stillness, seemed to speak from a distant world. Pärt had, in fact, spent his time in retreat studying Gregorian chant and the polyphonic music of the twelfth century composers of the school of Notre Dame in Paris (Pérotin et al.), and had come to the conclusion that the triad was the proper basis of music. (His earlier music had been serial.) He had also discovered a liking for the sound of bells and the art of change-ringing. In Pärt's new style, simple modal melodic lines, not unlike plainchant in their largely conjunct movement, were combined, note against note, solely with the pitches of the relevant triad. It was the constant presence of these pitches, as though emanating from the striking of a bell, which gave the music its static, timeless quality, furnishing the term 'tintinnabuli' to describe the process.[24]

One particularly captivating development of this technique was the placing of the triadic notes alternately above and below, and close to, the notes of the principal melody, resulting in some exquisite dissonances which, nevertheless, sound completely natural and inevitable, owing to the logic of the process.

The major work from this period, and the one which sums up most of Pärt's compositional concerns at this time, is undoubtedly **Tabula Rasa** (1977), a two-movement concerto grosso for two violins, string orchestra and prepared piano. The title ('clean slate') is perhaps symbolic of the new direction Pärt's music was taking. Certainly, the first movement's opening gesture, the two solo violins tearing off their lowest and highest A respectively, followed by a long silence, would seem to suggest this.

These two elements also turn out to be thematic. The note A grows into an alternately ascending and descending scale on the notes of the Aeolian mode on A, by the gradual addition of one note in each direction. Each note is colored by a tintinnabuli note, the resulting 2-part texture also being treated canonically, descending through the orchestra and returning to the starting point. After each addition of pitches to the scale there is a silence. As the scales get longer, so the silences get correspondingly shorter. The image is thus one of silence being gradually swallowed up by sound (music). The whole process is remarkably transparent, its slow unfolding readily perceivable by the listener.

The simplicity of the musical material and the somewhat mechanical way the scale pattern unfolds reminds one of some of Reich's early pieces, hence the subsequent labelling of Pärt as a minimalist, though it seems unlikely that he was influenced by the new American music.

Pärt's volte-face, and the success of minimalism generally, became emblematic of a new anti-modernist, specifically anti-serialist, sensibility. Other Europeans who turned their backs on the international serial style to embrace a return to a more "accessible" language include Penderecki and Henryk Górecki (b.1933), who scored a spectacular success with his **3rd Symphony (Symphony of Sorrowful Songs)** of 1976.

Even the experimental music of England moved into calmer waters. The so-called "systems music" of John White (b.1936) and others is a specifically English take on minimalism; wry, ironic, self-effacing, disarmingly simple and often gently humorous. Another English composer, John Tavener (b.1944), now perhaps unfortunately bracketed with Pärt and Górecki but unquestionably representative of the new sensibility, if not really a minimalist, has nailed his colors to the mast of the Orthodox Church, his work a simple expression of his faith.

The success of minimalism placed a huge question mark over the wisdom of the serialists of the 50s in wanting to reinvent music. These latter saw minimalism as a retreat into a simplistic superficiality.

Philip Glass answered for the minimalist camp in deriding Darmstadt serialism as "crazy creepy music". It is clear that Glass, Reich et al saw their music as a reaction against serialism as well as a development of experimental music, and whatever else it may have done, minimalism gave the green light to the reinstatement of older, conventional concerns of musical organization, such as tonality and pulse, which the serialists hoped they had done away with for ever.

It should perhaps be added as a rider here that the green light was for the benefit of the avant-garde, since there were still many composers who saw themselves as continuing the great traditions of the past, writing as though Darmstadt, Cage and minimalism had never existed.

4
Responses

Tippett, Carter, Stravinsky

Michael Tippett was more responsive to the new, post-Darmstadt sound-world (though not the methodology), as can be seen in the sudden appearance of spiky textures, more disjunct melodic movement and harsh dissonance in his work of the 1960s. His opera **King Priam** (1958–61) is a case in point and makes a fascinating comparison with his previous essay in this genre, the warm and generously lyrical **The Midsummer Marriage**, completed in 1952. This is not to suggest that Tippett's lyrical sense was sacrificed but, under pressure from the "progressive" elements, it certainly became more distended and his style generally more expansive.

A similar move had previously been effected by the American composer Elliott Carter (b. 1908). A passionate enthusiast for all forms of modern art, Carter soon abandoned the neo-classicism of his early career in favor of a synthesis of European modernism with the American experimental tradition stemming from Ives, whom Carter had known as a young man, and from whom he developed his technique of simultaneous layers of contrasting musical material. But, where Ives employs simultaneity for descriptive purposes (a realization of what happens in life), for Carter it has no such programmatic connotations.

To create dynamic movement, Carter fashioned his celebrated technique of metric modulation, where, say, a quarter-note (crotchet) as part of a triplet becomes a new pulse.

The early 50s saw Stravinsky, by now an American citizen, perform what turned out to be his final change of direction as he began to adopt serialism, encouraged by his American friend Robert Craft's enthusiasm for Webern. The short chamber work **In Memoriam Dylan Thomas** (1954), in which a setting of the poet's 'Do not go gentle' for tenor and string quartet is framed by what Stravinsky calls Dirge Canons, where the strings are joined by 4 trombones, is based entirely on a 5-note cell but is firmly situated in the composer's neo-classical idiom.

Soon, however, Stravinsky moved closer to the more abstract sound-world of Webern and Boulez (he had expressed admiration for **Le marteau sans mâitre**). That influence is felt most strongly in **Movements for Piano and Orchestra** (1958–9) which, despite a few telltale signs in the orchestration, is one of Stravinsky's least individual works. It could be argued, justifiably, that Stravinsky's adoption of serialism was simply another of his re-inventions of historical styles but the impersonal character of advanced serialism makes any attempt to parody and personalize it almost impossible and this particular chapter in Stravinsky's journey through musical history is the least successful.

New Complexity

For the last quarter of the twentieth century, High Modernism (the legacy of Darmstadt) has been at the crossroads. Even if it may not be the international force the composers of the 50s hoped it would be, the belief in "progress" is as strong as ever and much challenging and confrontational work is still being produced. At the same time, other developments have taken place, shunting High Modernism away from the leading edge and into the general mainstream.

The composers grouped under the banner of so-called "New Complexity", mostly British though hardly constituting a school as such, represent the continuation of this progressive wing of modernism. They include Brian Ferneyhough (b.1943), Michael Finnissy (b. 1946), James Dillon (b.1950), Chris Dench (b.1953), and Richard Barrett (b.1959), The "complexity" resides in the incredible density of texture, rather than the "pointillism" of before, which these composers generally favor.

This is often achieved by simultaneous multi-layering of different strands of material, themselves of considerable complexity. The techniques employed include irrational note-values and subdivisions of the measure and various extended techniques, including multiphonics, microtones and unorthodox methods of articulation.

In his **Unity Capsule** for solo flute (1975–6), Ferneyhough asks the player to combine these and other devices at the same time, notating each one in great detail. An extract from the score is given below (Example 21).

Ex.21 Ferneyhough, Unity Capsule, p.14

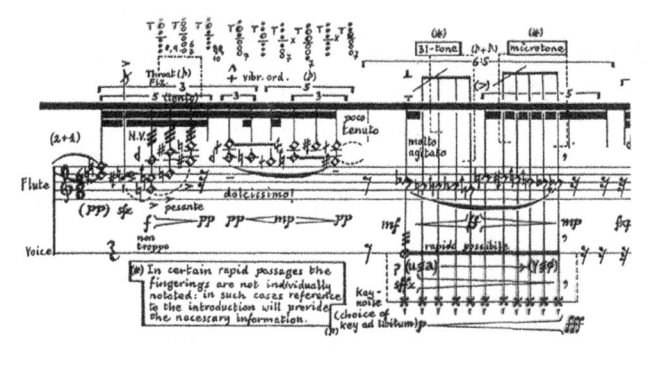

© Hinrichin Edition – Peters Edition Limited, London. Reprinted by permission of Peters Edition Limited, London

Intriguingly, Ferneyhough does not expect perfection of execution! The possibility of failure adds, for him, an extra dimension to the music, feverishly teetering as it is on the extreme edge of virtuosity.[25]

XENAKIS

At times, the overall impression, as well as the manner, of the music of these composers may resemble the micro-polyphony of Ligeti or the intricacies of Nancarrow though a more potent influence, particularly on the younger composers, is that of Iannis Xenakis (1922–2001). (Dench also cites the example of Ives.)[26] Xenakis's background as mathematician, architect and engineer ensured that, when he took up composition in the 1950s, the result would be a music of fierce originality and independence. Its massive quality owes much to Varèse but the real, and notorious, novelty lies in Xenakis's working out of the details of his textures by the use of probability theory and other constructs from the world of higher mathematics and science.

In this, he stood diametrically opposite to Cage's indeterminacy and use of chance. The results, though, sound anything but contrived or artificial. The music has a raw, physical power and, increasingly in the later works, a primitive quality, which can assault both the ears and the nerves of the listener though there is no denying the sheer excitement of the experience. This is as true of instrumental works like **Eonta** (1963–4) for piano and five brass instruments as it is for electro-acoustic pieces such as **Bohor** (1962) with its unremittingly loud wall of sound.

Spectralism

A fascination with sound, whether via complex texture or the raw material itself, has continued to exert a hold on composers during the greater part of the twentieth century. The eastern European composers of the 60s have already been discussed. French composers too have consistently shown a special aptitude for timbral subtlety and it is in France that the means for further exploration of the possibilities of sound itself has appeared.

During the 1970s, Boulez persuaded the French government to subsidize the establishment of an institution dedicated to research into the whole field of sound. Thus came into being the Institut de Recherche et Coordination Acoustique/Musique (IRCAM) and it has attracted researchers and composers from all over the world by virtue of its state-of-the-art facilities and expert support. IRCAM's computers provide the ability to analyse the inner life of sound, its overtone content (spectrum), and to transform it in different ways, opening up many new possibilities for composition, both instrumental and electro-acoustic.

Leading figures in this movement are the Frenchmen Tristan Murail (b.1947) and Gérard Grisey (1946–98). Both composers were pupils of Messiaen, whose ideas on harmony and added resonance have played their part in shaping the direction of their work. In Murail's piece **Désintégrations** (1982–3) all the harmonic material is derived from the overtone contents of the instruments of the 17-piece ensemble. This is reinforced by synthetic sounds from the same source, generated by computer and recorded onto tape.

In a similar vein, the English composer Jonathan Harvey (b.1939) based his tape piece **Mortuos Plango, Vivos Voco** (1980) on the sounds of his son's treble voice and the great bell at Winchester Cathedral (the Latin title is part of the inscription on the bell; "I weep for the dead, I call the living…"). These two sounds are heard in their original state and also synthesized by the IRCAM computer. Furthermore, Harvey has the sounds take on each other's harmonic spectra, the whole piece thus being an exploration of the interface between the real and the synthetic.

This particular concern inhabits the work of the Finnish composer Kaija Saariaho (b.1952), a former student of Ferneyhough, now resident in Paris.

Saariaho clearly identifies with French culture, working frequently at IRCAM, and has absorbed something of that Gallic sensibility in the field of timbre/texture, resulting in compositions which display a sure delight in the handling of sonic transformation, the electronics blending effortlessly with the instrumental sound, often obscuring the boundaries between them.

That experience at IRCAM can influence the composition of pure instrumental music may be observed in the work of the younger English composer George Benjamin (b.1960). He too has a special fondness for French music and culture, developed early on in his career and blossoming especially during his studies with Messiaen and subsequent contact with Boulez and Murail. Benjamin had already completed a small but impressive group of instrumental pieces which illustrated his acute ear for sonority before Boulez invited him to work at IRCAM. The result was **Antara** (1985–87), a piece for ensemble and computerized keyboards which are used to transform the recorded sound of pan-pipes (Antara is an Inca word for the instrument). Perhaps influenced by the culture of the pan-pipes, the work is powerful and rhythmically exciting, in strong contrast to the impressionist washes of sound characteristic of many spectral scores.

In any case, there is much more to Benjamin's music than the above commentary might suggest. While slowly unfolding, exquisitely imagined soundscapes are a common feature of his work, from **Ringed by the Flat Horizon** (1980), his first major orchestral work, through to **Sudden Time** (1989–93), a later addition to that repertoire, Benjamin is quite capable of more overtly dramatic statements, as in the youthful though astonishingly assured **Piano Sonata** (1977–8) or the later **Viola, Viola** (1997), a gritty, uncompromising and fiercely virtuosic duet for that instrument.

The composer himself has often said that considerations of harmony are at least as important to him as any other parameter. This does not, of course, mean functional harmony as traditionally understood, but it does indicate a concern with the way harmonies make a continuity. The problem for Benjamin, as for many other composers in comparable situations, is that he works entirely intuitively, rather than with any system.

It is not surprising, therefore, that his harmonic language is so bound up with his ear for sonority. In this respect he is close to Debussy and Messiaen. The latter's influence can certainly be detected in places (both the **Piano Sonata** and **Ringed by the Flat Horizon** contain echoes of the exuberant side of Messiaen) but without the benefit of a modal system or a highly developed sound – color synaesthesia Benjamin is totally reliant on his ear and his experience. Even Debussy, for all the freedom that he exhibited, had the good old tonal system behind him.

5
PIONEERS COME OF AGE

LATER FELDMAN

ALTHOUGH NEVER LINKED WITH OTHER texturalist composers, probably because of his association with Cage and the experimental tradition, there is no denying the surface beauty of Morton Feldman's music. (John Cage once lamented that it was "too beautiful".)[27] The way in which Feldman releases, as it were, his sounds, whether single notes, chords or noises, into the air and into time, forces one to listen entirely in the present and savor their essence. Feldman had maintained a great interest in the work of the abstract expressionist painters of 1950s New York, as already noted, and this was largely instrumental in his coming to regard a score as a canvas, the sounds arranged over it as though they were dabs of color. The repetition of small motifs in different contexts, or with minute variation, greatly enhances this analogy.

This patterning approach to composition, which grew naturally out of Feldman's earlier, freer, method took on greater significance during the last decade or so of his life as he began a serious study of near-Eastern, especially Turkish, rug making. What fascinated Feldman was the technique employed, whereby ostensibly repeated patterns in the weave would in fact be inexact or asymmetrical.

Asymmetrical repetition became one of the key elements in Feldman's work as did his tendency to allow the repetitions to continue for as long as was felt necessary. This might be a very long time indeed and in some of his last works, Feldman entered into time scales of Noh-like proportions. **For Philip Guston**, a chamber work from 1984 dedicated to one of Feldman's favorite painters, lasts 4 hours.

One of the omnipresent qualities of Feldman's music is the sheer immediacy of the sounds. No matter whether they arrive singly or in patterns, their unsullied nakedness can be disconcerting to the listener, precisely because there is nothing else. Feldman's oft-quoted answer to Stockhausen's probing to explain his secret was that he did not "push the sounds around".[28] In this, Feldman was, of course, closer to Cage and it is interesting to observe a somewhat Feldmanesque complexion in the sound-world of Cage's late works, the so-called "number" pieces.

Later Cage

In these pieces, for varying sizes of ensemble (the number of players furnishing the title in each case), each sound is placed within a time-bracket the beginning and end of which is flexible. Its duration is free as long as it does not exceed the limits of the time-bracket. The pieces exhibit a certain floating quality reminiscent of Feldman though there is much more interpenetration of sounds, especially where the ensemble is large. Cage pronounced himself happy with this new technique, which also enabled him quickly to fulfil the many commissions which continued to come in. It is tempting to view the tranquillity of these pieces as indicative of a "final period" in Cage's career but, as ever, there is no guarantee that another change of direction was not round the corner, once the possibilities of this manner had exhausted themselves.

The pieces are, nevertheless, in stark contrast to Cage's work of the 70s and 80s, which are characterized by the experimentation, part mischievous, part innocent, that one usually associates with the figure of John Cage. In a curious tilt towards post-modernism, some of this experimentation was with existing music; hymn tunes (**Hymns and Variations** (1979)), operas (the five **Europeras** of 1985–91), the music of Satie (**Cheap Imitation** (three versions from 1969–77)).

Other works revived the spirit of the multi-media event or happening, now termed a "circus". In **Roaratorio** (1979), subtitled An Irish Circus on Finnegans Wake, Cage himself read from Joyce's novel, accompanied by tapes of sounds recorded at places mentioned in the book, together with excerpts of Irish folk music played either live or recorded on tape. The I Ching was used to determine many of the performance details.

Cage had become, by this stage, very much in demand, even popular, albeit that his unpredictability and protean creativity remained undimmed. Having once led the (or an) avant-garde, he was now in the curious position of having lived through the period of its greatest influence. By the time of his death in 1992, his particular brand of experimentation had long been unfashionable, which makes his commitment even more remarkable.

LATER STOCKHAUSEN

Stockhausen, likewise, in later life, showed no sign of letting up though, unlike Cage, he still remained committed to the idea of a musical universe united by some sort of formula. This, rather than "series", became the preferred term for Stockhausen, since it could be of any constitution and could generate all the material of a composition.

The formula for **Mantra**, for two pianos and electronics (1970) is a complex mixture of melodic and rhythmic motifs, and was helpfully drawn by the composer on the front cover of the original LP recording. Stockhausen's immense cycle of seven operas, **Licht** (Light), which occupied him from 1977 until 2003, has three formulae, one for each of the principal characters, prompting comparisons with Wagner. Here, though, the comparison ends, for Stockhausen's treatment of his formulae is static rather than symphonic and each opera is a loose collection of different pieces, related in content but avoiding any narrative. More critically, Stockhausen replaces Wagner's timeless, universal mythology with one rooted in his own family and entourage – his favored, almost his only, performers for the past quarter of a century.

REVISIONS

Another great figure of post-war modernism, Pierre Boulez, has been productive in an entirely different way, revising his earlier scores and, as is well known, spending more time conducting other music. He has, though, taken more advantage of the facilities at IRCAM than hitherto. The instantaneous transformation of sound that is one of the prime features of that institution's computers is explored in **Dialogue de l'ombre double** (1985), for solo clarinet, the 'double shadow' of the title referring to the electronic image of the soloist heard through the loudspeakers.

This piece, though, has its roots in an earlier work for clarinet, **Domaines** (1961–8), which itself exists in two versions: for solo clarinet and for clarinet plus six small ensembles. Like the vocalist in Berio's **Circles**, the clarinet, in this second version, moves around the groups, sharing material with them.

It is the nature of Boulez's approach that a composition can be continually revised and, by implication, may never reach its final form. It is always a work-in-progress. This appears to be the situation with **Pli selon pli**, a portrait of Mallarmé, which first appeared in 1962 after five years of preparation, but has undergone countless revisions since. A composition may also be the source for further pieces where Boulez detects possibilities for development along related lines. Thus **Domaines** can be considered the 'parent' work to **Dialogue de l'ombre double**.

A particularly spectacular instance of Boulez' revisionism concerns the **Douze notations**, a little-known set of twelve miniatures for piano from 1945, which Boulez began to orchestrate and extend in 1977 and which, now simply titled **Notations**, have been transformed into a much more substantial piece, though again it would be unwise to consider it finished.

The idea that a work can engender other works is something that also preoccupied Berio, as can be seen in the collection of **Sequenzas** (1958–2004), each for a different solo instrument (No 3 is for female voice). Although basically monodic pieces, the **Sequenzas** contain harmonic and other implications which allowed Berio to expand some of them into a new series of ensemble and orchestral pieces entitled **Chemins**, a project which occupied him from 1964 to 1996.

The process continues even within the new series itself, **Chemins III** (1968) being an elaboration of **Chemins II** (1967), which in turn is derived from **Sequenza VI** for solo viola (1967). Some of the **Sequenzas** exist in more than one version. The last of them, **Sequenza XIV** for cello (2002), was later transcribed for double bass, not by Berio, however, but by the virtuoso Italian bassist Stefano Scodanibbio (b.1956).

One variety of revisionism, not uncommon in the second half of the twentieth century, is the turning away from progressive or avant-garde tendencies in order to revisit compositional problems of a previous age, often with their associated language. This may have more to do with an apparent disillusionment with progressive modernism than a reinvention of the past as seen, for example, in Stravinskyan neoclassicism. Or it may be a case of a composer finding fresh relevance in procedures and techniques which were assumed to be of no further significance in the modern world.

The inevitable targets are the symphony and its relatives i.e. the string quartet, sonata and so on. Attempts to weld the structure to non-functional harmony, atonality or serialism have usually been beset with difficulties, so deeply tied as it is to long-range harmonic relationships. This does not mean that the problem is insurmountable but it does present the composer with an enormous challenge.

Returning to tonality is one option and this has been the choice of Penderecki, who first made moves in this direction in his **St Luke Passion** (1963–66). It subsequently made possible the series of symphonies he began in 1973. (As of this writing, eight have been completed.)

The appearance of a symphony from the pen of Peter Maxwell Davies would have once been thought unlikely, if not inconceivable. Yet there is plenty of evidence of an ability to construct lengthy musical arguments with the magic square technique he had developed. His **Symphony No.1** duly arrived in 1976 and marked the start of a remarkably varied series of essays in the genre, culminating in 2000 with the **Symphony No. 8 (Antarctic).**

Davies's solution to the tonal problem was less extreme than Penderecki's in that he sought to adapt his existing technique to create a language in which modality, mediaeval rhythmic devices, tonality and atonality could coexist and produce the kind of harmonic tension required. One noticeable difference, however, was a lessening of the expressionism of his earlier work in favor of a warmer, more romantic, sound-palette.

This is partly due to Davies's increasing responsiveness to the landscape and culture of Orkney, to where he had moved in 1971, but one should also take into account the compositional models which inspired him, notably Sibelius, whose masterly symphonic technique is consistently held up as a paradigm of the highest standard by latter-day symphonists. Sibelius's motivic concentration, for example in the **Fourth Symphony** (1911), and his highly sophisticated art of transition, seen throughout his work, are techniques readily adaptable to almost any style and their integration into Davies's methodology has been immensely beneficial.

Since his pioneering work with The Fires of London, Davies has enjoyed close and fruitful associations with the BBC Philharmonic Orchestra and the Scottish Chamber Orchestra and it may be argued that working for such prestigious ensembles can also be responsible for developing a sympathetic handling of orchestral resources.

In Davies's case, it has produced a further, rather unexpected, result; the composition for the SCO of the ten **Strathclyde Concertos** (1987–95) for assorted soloists, duos and, in the last of the series, a wind sextet. The strong echoes of Bach's **Brandenburg Concertos** is clearly deliberate, Davies taking his position with the orchestra seriously and acting as a veritable Kapellmeister.

6
OTHER RESPONSES

LACHENMANN

THE IMMEDIACY OF SOUNDS, NOTED above in connection with Feldman, takes on a slightly different meaning when one is faced with the music of Helmut Lachenmann (b.1935). His starting point was, firstly, the integral serialism of Boulez, Stockhausen and, especially, Nono, in many ways the purest, most ascetic of the Darmstadt generation, and secondly, the timbral composition which emerged in the 60s.

The importance of Nono for Lachenmann lay in his (Nono's) ontological attitude to sound, its production and deployment, before any considerations of note-rows or themes. The closeness of Nono's work to the discoveries of the composers of timbral music was what set Lachenmann on his path. It is principally a concern with the physicality and acoustic quality of sound (a concern also shared by Varèse several decades previously), and not for nothing is Lachenmann's music labelled "musique concrète instrumentale". As with classic musique concrète, it is often difficult to tell what a sound is or what is producing it.

Lachenmann's most celebrated work is probably **Mouvement (-vor der Erstarrung)** (1983–4). The "movement" is constant and active, giving the impression of a hidden narrative, but it is all illusory, producing only stasis and torpidity (Erstarrung). The composer refers to this as an "Angst-ridden attempt to strike water out of the stone of the dead monument known as 'music'".[29]

Lachenmann's fundamentalism thus subverts the post-war serialists' attempts at a fresh beginning for music, seen now as something of a dead end, no further development along those lines being possible – hence the above quotation. One can hear echoes of Lachenmann's revolt against revolt in the work of many younger composers, among whom Rebecca Saunders (b.1967) stands out as one of great potential. Like Lachenmann, Saunders works with basic sounds, including the noise element associated with sound production, and small gestures such as microtonal and timbral deviations. These techniques are also the concern of spectralists like Saariaho but Saunders's sounds have less of the sensuousness of those composers, more a grittiness and physicality as if they were ready to jump off the page and be touched.

SCELSI

Yet another type of fundamentalism is found in the work of Giacinto Scelsi (1905–88) who, despite belonging to an older generation, did not receive any wide recognition until the 1980s and even today still remains a somewhat shadowy figure. Scelsi confined his approach to a reduced vocabulary of pitches, the most famous, and extreme, example being the **Quattro pezzi (su una nota sola)** (1959). The title (Four Pieces on a Single Note) says it all; one pitch subjected to continuous microtonal, dynamic and timbral deviation. Scelsi was inspired by various non-Western cultures, particularly those of the Orient, whose often static music clearly influenced his own.

Many of the titles of his pieces, as well as the texts of those for vocal and choral forces, have strong oriental resonances and employ words and phonemes from sacred traditions such as the Buddhist and Vedic. Thus in the choral and orchestral piece **Konx-om-pax** (1969), the middle syllable is a sacred sound associated with Tibetan Buddhism. On the other hand, 'pax' is, of course, Latin and is associated with Catholicism, the mystical side of which was also of interest to Scelsi.

YOUNGER GERMANIC COMPOSERS

Lachenmann's influence on German, and German-speaking, composers is, as one might expect, considerable and it has been interesting to observe the emergence of a sizeable number of them in recent years. This is not to suggest that they are all imitators of Lachenmann, rather that the older composer has forced a radical rethink on the part of the younger generations as to the very nature and meaning of composition at this period in the continuing fraught development of contemporary 'serious' music.

Representative of this newer generation is Wolfgang Rihm (b.1952), now old enough to be regarded as something of a figurehead, especially in view of his astonishingly large output. Rihm refuses to acknowledge any system of composition as more viable than any other, espousing instead total spontaneity. This means that suggestions thrown up during the creative process can literally lead anywhere; to totally original continuities or even to references to other musics. Style is not fixed. This is not to imply, however, that Rihm's music lacks shape or coherence; quite the reverse. The evidence is of a sustained dialogue between composer and material; the former willing the latter into ever more surprising configurations, the latter reminding the former of what its possibilities for development are.

The element of surprise is particularly strong in Rihm's work, keeping the listener on the edge of his or her seat, yet there is also a sense of direction, such as is often experienced with great jazz improvisers, giving the impression that the dual partnership of composer and material is working productively.

In the long fourth section of Rihm's **Frage** for mezzo soprano and ensemble (1999–2000), this mixture of surprise and inevitability is apparent in the concentrated exploration of the low sounds of the ensemble (bass clarinet, cor anglais, double bass, piano, percussion) which are invested with an explosive energy and physicality.

Rihm has, like Berio and Boulez, been drawn towards the idea of continuous composition, every new piece being derived in some way from preceding ones. The methodologies of all three composers are, in fact, quite similar, though Rihm is, if anything, more prodigal with his self-borrowing. New layers are grafted on to older pieces and a layer may subsequently acquire a separate existence as a piece in its own right but may then have new layers added to it, and so on. The composition of **Frage** is the result of a series of maneuvers of this sort, the chronology of which becomes totally meaningless since, in a sense, Rihm is continually revising the same piece.

Rihm's influence can be felt in the music of Matthias Pintscher (b.1971). He too prefers to work intuitively, being guided by whatever his opening idea seems to suggest in the way of continuation. His **Five Pieces for Orchestra** (1997), for example, are superficially reminiscent of the sound-world of the Second Viennese School, evidently by virtue of the title alone, so closely associated with that illustrious group. But Pintscher's expressionism, clearly apparent in this work, is naturally wider in scope than is that of his predecessors and seems more central to his style as a whole.

Rihm's near contemporary, Beat Furrer, born in Switzerland in 1954, has also been attracted to the fundamentalist ethic referred to above, but exploring more esoteric notions like the "space" between silence and the first intimation of a sound's appearance.

In some works, especially those involving voices and percussion, Furrer can achieve a near-inaudibility which makes Feldman's music seem deafening by comparison. But there is a feverishness in Furrer's music, rather than a Feldmanesque serenity, which always threatens to boil up to the surface and explode – as indeed often happens. Furrer has also developed other unusual ideas, such as the negation of the commonly held view of music as a linear process, unfolding in time. He has posited the notion of a composition being a magnification of a single instant (the Now), with all the details happening simultaneously.

These details are mostly, of necessity, small repetitive motifs or sequences of sounds. The listener experiences the music, as it were, vertically, as a constant process of transformation, different layers of the total sound becoming exposed then sinking back to be replaced by others, though never entirely disappearing.

A powerful example of Furrer's method is **Nuun** (1996), for two pianos and orchestra, a piece built from a teeming mass of scurrying figures, shooting arpeggios and irregular crescendos and diminuendos on held notes, anchored by hammered out B naturals on the pianos. The texture is both static and dynamic, the rhythmic complexity creating real momentum. There is even a sense of finality as the texture evaporates towards the end and the pianos, playing bare fourths, fifths and octaves, climb steadily upwards to a B natural – their starting point.

7
REFERENCE AND QUOTATION

REFERENCES TO AND QUOTATIONS OF other music have become defining features of what is now post-modernism, this vast ocean in which anything is possible, anything can be legitimized and everything is everybody's business. Referentialism, to use an all-inclusive term, is not in itself anything new but during the course of the twentieth century it has become, for many composers, more and more part and parcel of the general fabric of musical discourse. There are obviously many ways in which pre-existing music can be used, from the blatant to the disguised, from the artless to the imaginative. Almost invariably, a degree of irony or playfulness is present, a trait already prefigured in some of the music of Poulenc.

In the early part of the century, as we have shown, quotation was central to Ives's transcendentalism and reference, if not actual quotation, was the main thrust of neo-classicism. In many ways, these examples strikingly anticipate post-modern practice. Ives insisted, for example, that the famous motif of Beethoven's **Fifth Symphony**, for which he had an obsession, was so full of possibilities that it should be allowed further development in the hands of other composers.

So we find, in the third movement *("The Alcotts")* of his **Concord Sonata**, the motif transformed into a piece of sentimental parlour-room piano music, transposed up a fifth and harmonized in B flat *major*. To some ears, this may appear disrespectful and irreverent, like Chabrier's infamous **Souvenirs de Munich (Quadrille on themes from Wagner's Tristan und Isolde)** (1885–6), but Ives is giving us a truthful picture of the kind of musical evenings round the piano which nineteenth century families like the Alcotts invariably spent.

Ives's position is clear (whether one approves of it or not), but there are isolated instances of quotation among composers to whom it was not normal practice which have often aroused controversy. One notorious example is Shostakovich's **Fifteenth Symphony** (1971) which blatantly quotes the spirited main theme from Rossini's **William Tell Overture** as well as the 'Destiny' motif from Wagner's **Der Ring des Nibelungen**.

The Rossini quotation seems playful, perhaps suggested by the general mood being created by the music's progress (not unlike the way some jazz musicians weave quotations into their improvisations), except that, after repeating the quotation a few more times, the playfulness wears off and and a more disturbing atmosphere takes over. Wagner's motif, however, comes as a bit of a shock, appearing without warning right at the start of the last movement. The explanation that Shostakovich was preoccupied with death while working on this, his last symphony does not, however, ease the rather unsettling presence of this familiarly foreign material.

There are other quotations from Wagner in Shostakovich's **Fifteenth Symphony**, notably the first three notes (the love motif) from **Tristan und Isolde**, used whimsically as an anacrusis to an innocent sounding melody, but Shostakovich also includes an altered version of the famous melody which dominates the first movement of his own **Seventh Symphony** (Leningrad) of 1941. This is indeed ironic seeing that, earlier in his career, Shostakovich had found himself on the receiving end of a 'tribute' when this grimly-repetitive, mocking theme was mercilessly parodied by Bartók in his **Concerto for Orchestra** (1943). The steady build-up of Shostakovich's melody (the technique is not dissimilar to that used by Ravel in his **Bolero**), was meant to portray the march of the Nazis on Leningrad during the Second World War. Bartók was possibly aware of this – he had just heard the Symphony on the radio – but his response reads like a criticism of Shostakovich's literalism and failure to universalize his feelings.

Just as unsettling as Shostakovich's insertions of Rossini and Wagner are those which appear in Henze's **Tristan**, a work whose turbulent background has already been discussed.[30] Besides the perhaps expected quotation from Wagner's eponymous music-drama, the work also contains distortions on tape of Chopin's famous Funeral March from his **Bb minor Piano Sonata** (No.2) and a sudden, unexpected intrusion of the opening of Brahms's **First Symphony**. This latter is as surprising as the appearance of Wagner in Shostakovich, and equally as bizarre, though no doubt Henze had his reasons.

In the later twentieth century, referentialism illustrates the easy accessibility of music of all periods and all geographical locations; it is the badge of a cut and paste sampling mentality which seeks to democratize the whole of culture. In 1968, a particular piece of imaginative daring issued from the pen of Luciano Berio. This was his **Sinfonia**, whose third movement is constructed almost entirely of quotations. The bedrock is provided by the third movement (Scherzo) of Mahler's **Second Symphony** (1888–94), a vestige of which runs like a thread for the entire duration, sometimes becoming submerged, then clearer, but always discernible.

On top of this is a complex patchwork of quotations from the orchestral repertoire, some obvious, others more obscure, and including some from Berio himself! A third layer is another patchwork, this time of verbal quotations from various sources from Samuel Beckett to graffiti, declaimed by eight vocalists. The effect is analogous to the stream of consciousness technique of writers like Joyce and Woolf (Joyce's *Finnegans Wake* is an obvious model and inspiration).

This method of using the familiar can also be found in the work of Robin Holloway (b.1943), an English composer who proclaims a strong affinity with nineteenth and early twentieth century Romanticism and late Romanticism. Holloway has openly stated his regret at the directions music has taken since then ("it might have gone different... it could have taken that road") [31] and he has developed a technique where actual quotations sit alongside allusions and references to that lost world – gestures, harmonies and suchlike that might have been written by a composer of that period. Holloway's music may be viewed as a homage to an age he wished he had been part of and an aura of wistfulness inevitably hangs over it.

A feeling of longing also pervades the music of the Russian, Alfred Schnittke (1934–98) though, as the natural heir to Shostakovich and a witness to some profound changes in the socio-political climate of his country, this tends more to despair and a grim humor, as when, towards the end of his **Faust Cantata, "Seid nüchtern und wachet"** (1982–3), the gory description of Faust's death is set to a shockingly banal tango. An admirer of the Berio **Sinfonia**, Schnittke developed a similar technique which he referred to as "polystylistics", whereby different musical styles are combined in the same piece, something again anticipated by Poulenc.

Schnittke likes the resonance of gestures and mannerisms from the various historical periods, such as cadence figures or accompaniment patterns. The material is frequently distorted in different ways, typically by saturating it with clusters of semitones or quarter–tones, or with atonal or polytonal harmonies. His decision to pursue this path was both a reaction to the linguistic crisis of confidence after the Second World War and a result of his experiences in film music, where the technique of cut and paste is widely used and a familiarity with the whole history of music can be an advantage.

Schnittke's methods of distortion can become positively surreal, especially when applied to familiar material, as happens with his arrangement for violin and piano of the carol Silent Night (**Stille Nacht**) of 1978 (see Example 22).

Ex.22   Schnittke, Stille Nacht, fig 2

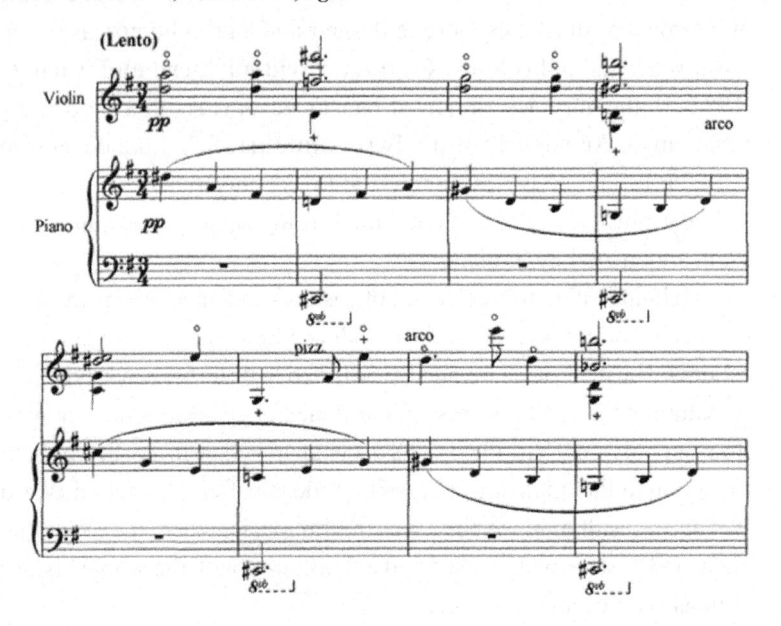

© Copyright 1978 by Musikverlag Hans Sikorski, HAMBURG. Reproduced by permission of Boosey & Hawkes Music Publishers Ltd.

Surrealism in music is not particularly common, but the distortion of the familiar, especially if exaggerated, and the juxtaposition of unrelated material can work equally well in music as in the visual arts. (In the realm of popular entertainment, the versions of popular classics and other material by the American bandleader Spike Jones (1911–65) frequently reached sublime levels, seldom if ever surpassed anywhere.) Peter Maxwell Davies's work of the 60s, already referred to above.[32] frequently took on a surreal edge as he developed his interest in the genre of music-theater. His **Missa super L'homme armé** (1968, rev.1971) uses distorted references to, among other things, 1920s popular music (a favorite of Davies') as well as the medieval tune of the title.

It must be admitted, however, that there seems to be a limit to the number of ways that distortion can be used before results become predictable, a criticism which could be levelled against the prolific output of Mauricio Kagel, whose unflagging dedication to the surrealist cause did not always preclude a degree of banality.[33]

Kagel's exploration of the jazz idiom in the chamber work **rrrrrrr…5 jazzstücke** (1981–2), part of a larger cycle of pieces investigating musical references with the letter 'r', is curiously flat and uninvolved, the specificity of the model clearly not inspiring the composer to his customary flight of extravagance and fantasy.

Kagel is on surer ground when giving form to his impressions of the sound-worlds of the eight main points of the compass in **Die Stücke der Windrose** (Compass Pieces), written between 1988–94 and scored for a 'salon' orchestra of clarinet, string quartet, double bass, piano, harmonium and percussion. Here, the creation of telling musical images is much more the work of the imagination and Kagel even manages to devise some novel sonorities out of this apparently limited instrumentation.

Something of Kagel's surrealistic humor can also be found in the music of his one-time pupil, the Irishman, Gerald Barry (b.1952) where, alongside extreme demands on stamina and virtuosity and a liking for fast tempi, it often takes on a manic quality. This is evident in two chamber works with graphic titles: '_____' and Ø (both 1979). The former is based on scalic material borrowed from Tchaikovsky, the latter on a system of ornamentation applied to an Irish folksong.

Central to Barry's output is opera, the libretto frequently subjected by the music's demands to a highly artificial, almost perverse, fragmentation. Phrases and even individual words become dislocated and their meaning obscured but the integrity of the melodic line remains. The primacy of melody over words is something of paramount importance to Barry, who cites Handel as an influence. (Repetition of text and florid melismas on single syllables are characteristics of the baroque *da capo* aria.) Barry's music is, in fact, notable for its insistence on line, in the sense of a continuity of expressive purpose, however fractured the general texture might be.

Opera also occupies a central position in the music of Judith Weir (b.1954) and, as in Barry, melody is crucial, though Weir's folksy, sing-song style is calculated to let the words be heard and understood. Her two-act but short (65 minutes) opera **Blond Eckbert** (1993) is typical. The plot, which is like an invented folk tale, unfolds in a manner both playful and matter-of-fact, precluding any empathy with the characters. The music, too, wears a mask of wry detachment, a trait which is found throughout her work, betraying the influence of the neo-classical Stravinsky. Tonal references abound, but they simply crop up during the course of the musical argument alongside other, more complex elements. Folk music itself is another strong presence, not only that of Scotland, the country of her family, but also that of the Balkans, an area with which she has developed a particular affinity. Folk music is not so much subsumed into her style as it is with Bartók, but rather commented upon in the same detached way.

An American contemporary of Weir, Michael Daugherty (b.1954) has achieved controversial notoriety through his series of "tribute" pieces to cultural icons of the United States. These range from theatrical chamber works like **Dead Elvis** (1993), where the eponymous rock 'n' roll star is portrayed by a suitably clad solo bassoonist, to **Le tombeau de Liberace** (1996), a mini piano concerto honoring the famous kitsch pianist, and even to an opera on the subject of one of the biggest of all female icons, **Jackie O** (1997). Daugherty's style is eclectic, inevitably referencing the music associated with his heroes, but though he keeps his tongue firmly, and probably respectfully, in his cheek, he cannot always avoid the temptation to overindulgence and the humor tends to pall.

8
OTHER CURRENTS

MACMILLAN, TURNAGE

IN REPLACING MODERNISM, EVEN IN all its variety, the post-modern world seeks to negate the idea of an avant-garde by suggesting that all procedures are acceptable and of equal value. Ironically, this allows an avant-garde or indeed any aspect of modernism to survive, though such survival may be regarded with suspicion since it clings to a world which has disappeared. Be that as it may, the situation at the end of the twentieth and beginning of the twenty-first centuries is just as complex and variegated as at any time during the last hundred years. Is it an aspect of post-modernism which is responsible for the plethora of individual styles still evident, or is this simply a continuation of what has always been the case?

Post-modernists may proclaim "the death of the author", but there are plenty of composers around who still adhere to the notion that writing music is an act of expressing some personal vision or philosophy. Nowhere is this more evident than in the music of James MacMillan (b.1959). A proud Scot and devout Catholic, MacMillan's art is an aspiring one; a seriousness of purpose lies behind even the more light-hearted secular pieces and his music always seems to be addressing some higher reality, inviting comparison with Messiaen and

J.S.Bach. Such commitment is rare nowadays and some may consider it pretentious, but one does not need to share MacMillan's faith to appreciate the vividness of the writing, its communicative power and sureness of touch, any more than one does with Messiaen and Bach.

MacMillan's self-confidence encourages a directness of expression which can be disconcertingly graphic, as in the percussion concerto **Veni, veni, Emmanuel** (1992) with its coda of unaccompanied bells or, even more explicitly, in **They saw the stone had been rolled away** (1993) for brass sextet and percussion, with its massive crescendi and thunderous effects.

Works like these mark MacMillan out as essentially a Romantic and, in common with others of similar persuasion, his style is eclectic. He can sift between the extremes of hard-edged modernism and simple tonal references as the occasion demands and the big, bold statements are balanced by moments of refined sensitivity.

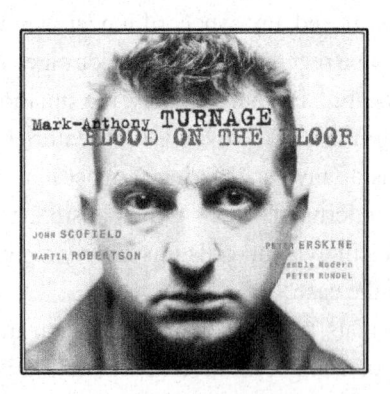

The directness of MacMillan's style is echoed in the work of his contemporary, Mark-Anthony Turnage (b.1960), though in his case it comes from a deep concern with contemporary social issues, and a love of jazz and black popular music. These show themselves in the aggressive edge apparent in much of Turnage's music, two early instances, both from 1988, being the ensemble piece **Release,** which features wailing saxophones, blaring brass and a percussion set-up including bits of scaffolding hit with a hammer and what Turnage calls "nasty-sounding ratchets", and the opera **Greek**, an updating of the Oedipus legend, set in the East End of London. The influence of jazz also informs Turnage's approach to harmony as well as his trademark fondness for the sound of the saxophone, especially the soprano, which always seems to symbolize the voice of alienation.

FURTHER USES OF JAZZ

Latterly, Turnage has begun to write more and more for jazz musicians playing and improvising alongside their "classical" colleagues. This practice, which harks back to the "Third Stream" movement, pioneered in the 1950s by Gunther Schuller (b.1925), John Dankworth (b.1927) and others, has always proved to be problematic, and Turnage has tried, in pieces like **Blood on the Floor** (1993–6), to avoid a chalk-and-cheese situation by having the two factions share a common linguistic basis. He has also been inspired by the 'orchestral' technique of big band writing employed by the American composer/arranger Gil Evans (1912–88) in his seminal recordings with jazz trumpeter Miles Davis (1926–91): **Miles Ahead** (1957), **Porgy and Bess** (1958) and **Sketches of Spain** (1959–60).

The magical partnership of Evans and Davis is one which has not escaped the attention of other sympathetic ears outside the jazz fraternity, one example being Simon Bainbridge (b.1952), whose short chamber work **For Miles** (1994) pays tribute not only to Davis's fragile and lonely sound (insofar as this is possible in a non-jazz piece) but also to the rhythmically intricate contrapuntal techniques for which Evans had a liking.

A more "inside" view is afforded by the **Concerto for Trumpet and Wind Orchestra** (1993), composed by Richard Rodney Bennett (b.1936) soon after he had learned of Davis's death. Bennett is himself a skilled practitioner in jazz, as both singer and pianist, and his knowledge and experience of the idiom is clearly responsible for the Concerto's closeness to the model. Bennett has had to face the problem of how to (or whether to) integrate the jazz and 'classical' sides of one's personality and solved it by keeping them separate.

Even so, there are moments, for example in his ensemble piece **Dream Dancing** (1986), one of a series of works based on Debussy's solo flute piece **Syrinx** (1912) (and also the title of a Cole Porter song!), where the harmony takes on a certain jazz flavor. Perhaps, though, Bennett, the one-time pupil of Boulez and composer of a number of challenging concert works, is showing where his sympathies really lie as well as unconsciously acknowledging the influential part that Debussy's harmonic language played in the evolution of jazz.

Bennett also enjoys success as a composer for films, indicating a third side to his personality. Remarkably, Bennett shows the same effortless fluency in this medium and a natural aptitude at producing music of fresh and appealing melodiousness which frequently recalls the now almost forgotten genre of British light music.

Ruders

Film music attracts another composer of distinct romantic leanings; the Dane, Poul Ruders (b.1949), but in his case the films are in his imagination (he has styled himself as "a film composer with no film"). Ruders's romanticism is of the expressionist kind, though he goes far beyond that of middle-period Schoenberg and Berg. Ruders writes music of breathtaking virtuosity, a veritable riot of invention, helped along in no small part by exploiting the extremes of the instruments' registers, particularly the high, and pushing the capabilities of the players to their utmost.

Ruders is in his element in the orchestral **Saaledes saae Johannes** (Thus saw St John), perhaps the archetypal Ruders piece, written in 1984 and inspired by the vision of Death on his pale horse, as recounted in the Book of Revelation. The work is certainly graphic, even gothic, yet Ruders manages to shy away from realistic picture painting and thus avoids any accusation of Hollywood style excess.

CONSERVATIVES

Reference has already been made to composers who have shunned the various avant-gardes that have come and gone, writing in what might seem a protective cocoon of sounds and gestures that belong to an age which has long disappeared. It is, in fact, one of the curiosities of the twentieth century that such a state of affairs persists. On the other hand, perhaps we should not be surprised, given that the century has always lacked a lingua franca and the different languages which have evolved have not found universal acceptance. There is also the fact that, for some, the whole business of being a composer and writing music has not changed since the nineteenth century, or even, in some cases, the eighteenth, and that all the aspects and branches of modernism have been nothing but temporary aberrations.

The music of Robert Simpson (1921–97), for example, bypasses pretty much the whole of modernism, keeping faith with the ideal of the great, established musical structures of the eighteenth and nineteenth centuries (symphony, string quartet) as vehicles for the large-scale dramatic working out of essentially musical problems, and, what is more, in an idiom which shows a clear relationship, in its adherence to tonal organization, with the music of the composers Simpson revered most: Beethoven, Bruckner and Nielsen. For Simpson, there was never an issue about musical language; the young Boulez's claim that serialism was the only language was so much hot air to Simpson who maintained an unshakeable belief in the strength and viability of tonality and its capacity to continue offering further possibilities to the composer.

Simpson's position is indeed remarkable and his impressive haul of eleven completed symphonies and (equalling Shostakovich) fifteen string quartets seems almost like an act of defiance, proclaiming the eternal truth of the sonata principle.

But as acts of defiance go, nothing quite compares with the massive orchestral work **Odyssey**, composed by Nicholas Maw (1935–2009). Clocking in at a staggering ninety six minutes, this continuous span of symphonic music, which occupied Maw from 1973 to 1987, is an audacious statement of belief in the power of traditional forms of expression. Maw is not so impervious to modernism as was Simpson, preferring to take what he needs from others while remaining firmly committed to the principle of tonality as the *sine qua non* of musical structure. Indeed, it is difficult to imagine **Odyssey** being achieved without some form of tonal organization.

Maw's cautionary attitude to modernism places him in the company of other British composers of his generation, including John McCabe (b.1939) and William Mathias (1934–92), as well as younger figures like David Matthews (b.1943). Their attitudes to tonality may differ considerably, but there is a shared allegiance to its power as a basic principle; what Maw describes as a 'fixed point'[34] from which, theoretically, anything can be related, not just functional harmonic progressions.

The figures of Benjamin Britten and Michael Tippett (particularly in his earlier work) would seem to be important models here, both composers enriching their essentially conservative styles with influences drawn from disparate sources ranging from Mahler and Berg to Stravinsky and, at least for Tippett, the blues and jazz.

The inventiveness with which Britten broadens the ambit of tonality, by calling upon a wide variety of techniques and devices, has always been an outstanding aspect of his style, permitting the creation of musical images of striking precision, particularly when allied to words or dramatic situations.

Thus we find, in **Curlew River** (1964), the first of the composer's Church Parables, freely superimposed layers of dissonant harmonies, tone clusters and heterophonically presented modal melody; techniques derived, at least in part, from the traditional music of Japan, the original inspiration for this most engaging of Britten's works.

A more common technique, which served Britten well in the exploration of his favorite themes of corruption and the loss of innocence, is the destabilising of a tonality by 'foreign' elements. Among dozens of instances, one particularly poignant example may be cited: in the setting of Wilfred Owen's poem *Strange Meeting*, towards the end of the **War Requiem**, the two dead soldiers recount their stories in a melodic line which floats chromatically and independently, following its own mysteriously logical path, over the static and slowly shifting G minor harmonies (marked 'cold') underneath. Despite the line's independence, Britten guides it carefully, brushing it against the harmonies in some beautifully contrived dissonances. Example 23 shows the German soldier's first phrase.

The way Britten builds the melody, basically a simple scale outlining a rising succession of perfect 4ths, to climax on a dissonant D flat is a perfect illustration of the kind of felicitous touch which one finds throughout his work. A third ingredient, heard in the first part of the narration where the British soldier first comes across his German counterpart, is the periodic interjection of string chords – last inversion dominant sevenths minus their fifths – articulated as a short crescendo *pp* to *f* and with vibrato. Like the melodic line, these chords are independent of the underlying tonality, all three layers combining in creating an image of desolation, which is made all the more effective by the relative simplicity of the materials used.

Ex.23 Britten, Strange Meeting (War Requiem), fig 121

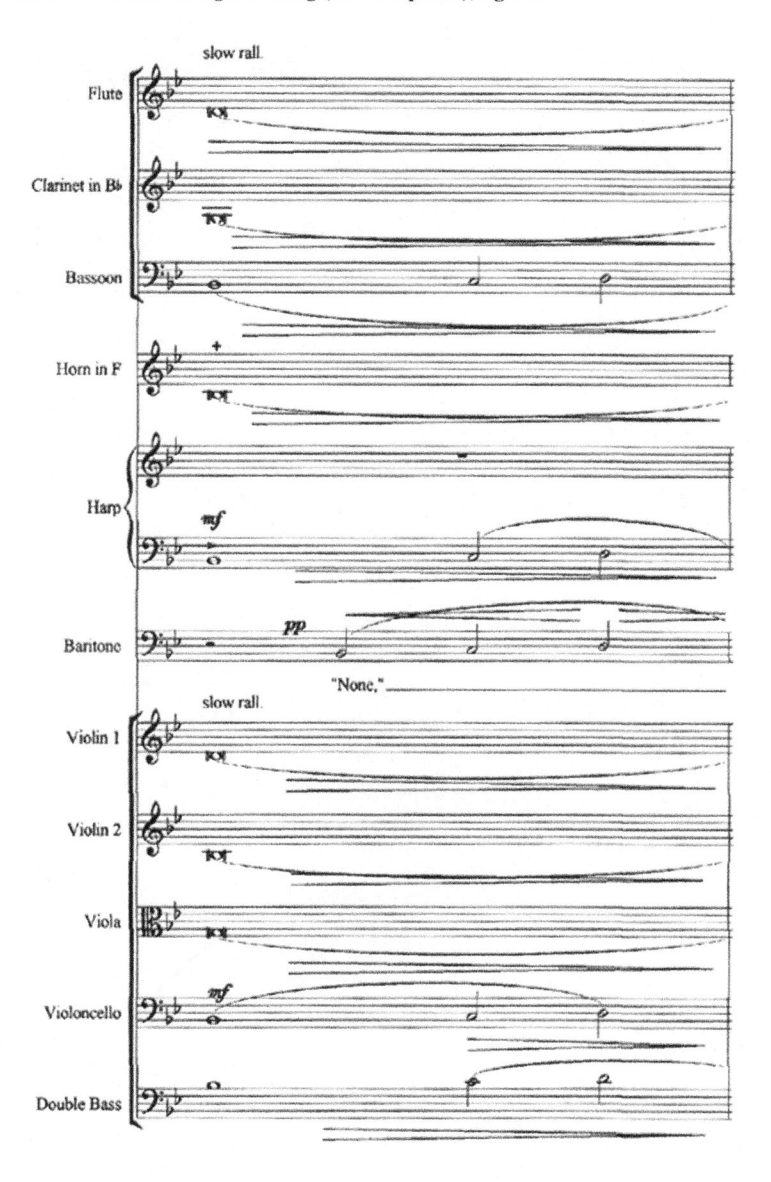

© Copyright 1961 by Boosey & Hawkes, Music Publishers Ltd. Reproduced by kind permission.

It is Britten's openness to all technical procedures, providing they serve the expressive purpose of the work in question, that is such an important lesson and it is instructive to note how pervasive his influence has been, especially bearing in mind that he did not take private pupils, never mind teach in an academic institution. But he did employ assistants, one of them being the afore-mentioned David Matthews, a composer who perhaps comes as close as anyone in inheriting Britten's mantle, most particularly with regard to the idea of the composer as craftsman, fulfilling a role in society and, without compromising himself, attempting to communicate as directly as possible with his audience.

This is, of course, the *Gebrauchsmusik* ideal of the 1930s which served Britten well during his life but, with the perception of the value of the "serious" composer in the late twentieth century having shifted dramatically, is less of a realistic ideal for Matthews and others like him.

In matters of technical procedure, Matthews is similarly wide-ranging, always putting the expressive demands before anything else. A Romantic by nature, he inclines to the larger musical structures, especially string quartet and symphony, but is strongly attracted to extra-musical (literary and visual) stimuli. In keeping with this characteristic, Matthews is deeply concerned with problems of harmonic movement and direction, which he tries to solve by reinterpreting some of the techniques of traditional tonal music. Matthews's **Fourth Symphony** (1989–90) uses the note B as a loose kind of tonic or reference pitch and features the device of steadily rising pedal points to create a feeling of inexorability, in a way reminiscent of the first movement of Nielsen's **Fifth Symphony**.

In his orchestral tone poem **In the Dark Time** (1984–5), Matthews makes use of what he calls a germinal chord, a self-explanatory term which can be understood as a more complex kind of tonic – a reference sonority. The chord, a second inversion B flat major triad with D and A major triads on top,[35] cannot really behave as a conventional tonic but it is rich in harmonic possibilities. One such forms the coda of the work, a short section which bears the key signature of D major (the only use of a key signature in the entire work), the harmony eventually coming to rest on the open 5th, A and E.

YOUNGER ENGLISH COMPOSERS

Matthews is one of a number of highly respected and gifted British composers of the 'post-Manchester school' generation, though their birth-years span three decades. Several of these have already been dealt with elsewhere in this book but we should also mention David Matthews's younger brother Colin (b.1946), Oliver Knussen (b.1952), Robert Saxton (b.1953), Christopher Fox (b.1955), Julian Anderson (b.1967) and Thomas Adès (b.1971). The sheer number of these composers makes one think of the English renaissance at the turn of the last century. However, this current outpouring of talent has not followed the lacuna that made the previous one so extraordinary, neither has any awakening of national consciousness united their endeavors and given them a sense of direction and purpose.

What can be detected, though, is a generally liberal, sometimes eclectic, attitude to all available modernisms and a particularly noticeable desire to embrace expressivity at the expense of abstraction, strong responses to visual, dramatic and literary stimuli being quite common. Above all, there is little sense of allegiance to a past avant-garde, which is not to say, however, that individual composers do not show a particular preference for one branch of modernism rather than another.

The survival of the gentle, sometimes ironic humor and objective devotion to process associated with the English and American experimental tradition may be observed, for example, in the work of Christopher Fox. Fox's musical sympathies and the reach of his ideas are, however, much wider than might be imagined, even taking in the rarefied world of post-war Darmstadt, where Fox himself has given lectures in recent years. He has, consequently, been able to move on from the rather restricted universe of 60s and 70s experimentalism, while still maintaining the delight in discovery which so typified that period.

Of this diverse group, Oliver Knussen stands out, not just as a composer of stature, but as a conductor of great insight and indefatigable champion of the works of his contemporaries and younger colleagues. Both Matthews brothers and Julian Anderson, as well as foreign composers such as Poul Ruders, have been notable beneficiaries of Knussen's generosity. Knussen also has a reputation for promoting the works of older composers in whom he has a special interest, such as Ives and Carter, creating an image of him as being cut from the same cloth as Pierre Boulez.

As a composer, Knussen is perhaps less eclectic than others, sharing with Boulez a continuing attraction to serial procedures, though not quite to the same extent as the older master. Of greater importance, however, is the rhythmic dexterity of Carter. Knussen's use of rhythm, rather than tonal relationships, to delineate musical ideas and to resolve contrasts between them owes something to Carter's example, but there is a muscularity and strong sense of narrative in Knussen's music which is more reminiscent of Stravinsky or Adams.

Another prominent figure is Thomas Adès, a precociously gifted composer and a conductor and pianist of distinction. Adès is blessed with a quite extraordinary aural imagination, evident even in his earliest works, like the ensemble piece **Living Toys** (1993), which reveals a confident handling of all sorts of technical procedures and instrumental possibilities, especially when fired by powerful visual images, like the child's fantastical world depicted in the afore-mentioned piece. This has led to some comparing him to the youthful Britten.

The comparison is not inapt but Adès's teeming imagination and wide musical sympathies have led him more in the direction of postmodern referentialism, except that he regards the references as not so much ironic comments on musical tradition but as a general celebration of it. This, of course, begs the question, for it can be extremely difficult, given the abstract nature of music, to decide one way or the other whether a given passage is ironic or celebratory. The answer will, in most cases, lie in the context, and there is certainly nothing in Adès which compares with the exaggeration and sheer wackiness one finds in, say, Kagel or Barry.

Indeed, as many commentators have noted, there is an underlying seriousness in Adès's music. Responses to it are more in the nature of open-mouthed astonishment and admiration than the raised eyebrow or half-smile.

9
WINDS FROM THE EAST

THE POST-WAR YEARS HAVE SEEN a number of composers from the Far East, principally China, Japan and Korea, establishing themselves in Europe and America, having been attracted by the latest developments taking place at the time, particularly those at Darmstadt. One of the first to gain an international reputation was Isang Yun (1917–95), who was born in South Korea but eventually settled in Germany. Yun attended the Darmstadt courses and also began to develop a strong political commitment. This was soon to land him in serious trouble with the Korean authorities who kidnapped him in Berlin and sent him back to Korea to be imprisoned. The international music community secured his release.

Yun's artistic mission was a synthesis of the western avant-garde and the traditional music of his native land. This blend of east and west was, for Yun, a symbolic act of unification, the sense of suffering yet feeling of warmth for humanity which pervades the music a clear response to Yun's experiences with the forces of oppression.

Of a rather different persuasion is Unsuk Chin (b.1961). Also from South Korea, Chin has established a reputation as a highly sophisticated colorist, a composer who tries "to render into music the visions of immense light and of an incredible magnificence of colors that I see in all my dreams".[36] Echoes perhaps of Messiaen, but Chin's music is closer, in its incredibly refined and subtle attention to detail, to composers like George Benjamin (who has, in fact, conducted her work) and the spectralists.

Chin is an example of an Oriental composer who has integrated herself completely into the ways of western new music. Unlike Yun, she seems not to be particularly interested in utilizing Korean traditional music in her work, or indeed showing any obvious aspect of oriental sensibility. But trying to quantify how much of their heritage goes into the artistic character of oriental composers is often difficult. The Japanese composers who, influenced by Cage and the Fluxus community, became part of the experimental scene during the 60s, such as Toshi Ichiyanagi (b.1933) and Takehisa Kosugi (b.1938), appeared to bring specifically Japanese qualities, such as stillness and a devotion to sound itself, to the work they produced, but these qualities were already in evidence in Cage's music. Ichiyanagi's **Anima 7**, which requires a chosen activity to be performed as slowly as possible, is pure Fluxus.

Tōru Takemitsu (1930–96), probably the most renowned of all Japanese composers, showed a distinct ambivalence towards the traditional music of Japan; its associations with the more unseemly side of nationalism, of which he had had some experience during the war, tempered slightly by an innate feeling for its fetching modality.

The negative side of this equation caused Takemitsu to turn his back on his country and he came increasingly under the spell of a wide range of western music, including jazz, pop and American show tunes.[37] His propensity towards modality drew him inevitably to Debussy and, especially, Messiaen, but he must also have recognized, in their contemplative, non-developing view of structure, a certain affinity with the traditional music of Japan.

Messiaen remained a powerful influence throughout Takemitsu's life, his unique modal-derived harmony being unashamedly plundered, but Takemitsu achieves a fluidity of rhythm and a sensuousness of texture which is more Debussyan in origin. Also typical are the self-contained phrases which follow one another in an improvisatory way, inviting the listener to contemplate them individually.

While this too may owe something to Debussy, it is a more overtly Japanese, specifically Zen, quality, adding to the general image of a kind of Japanese Impressionism. This image is particularly potent in the works on themes of water and rain, for example the ensemble pieces

Rain Spell (1982) and **Waterways** (1978) (where one can almost smell the moss!) and **riverrun** (1984) for piano and orchestra, one of a group of works inspired also by James Joyce's *Finnegans Wake*.

Many of Takemitsu's characteristics are echoed in the work of his young disciple Toshio Hosokawa (b.1955). His youthful attitude to the traditional music of Japan was one of active dislike and it was not until he had spent some time in Berlin studying western contemporary music (Isang Yun was one of his teachers) that his views changed. His music has since taken on a more pronounced Japanese quality showing the influence of, on the one hand, the playing techniques of Japanese instruments such as the shakuhachi, koto and shô and, on the other, the Zen-inspired approach to sound and silence (i.e. their mutual dependence). Once again however, Hosokawa realizes, and acknowledges, that these concerns have been occupying the attentions of Western composers since the 1950s and it is as much their influence that has brought this turnaround as it is his recognition of his own national identity. Such is the bizarre predicament of the contemporary Japanese composer.

Tan Dun (b.1957) came to the United States from China in 1987, having survived the Cultural Revolution then becoming acquainted with the music of the western avant-garde while still a student at the Beijing Conservatoire. Like Shostakovich under Stalinist repression, Tan found his music denounced as unsympathetic to the idealism of the musical establishment and he was forced to flee the country.

Tan's fusion of elements of traditional Chinese music with those of the western avant-garde is made more compelling by his striking flair for the visual and theatrical. This is seen at its best in works like the **Orchestral Theater** series, of which there are (so far) five (actually numbered 0–4). Written between 1990 and 1999, these pieces feature such novelties as the voices of the orchestral players, Chinese and Japanese opera singers and video projections. The **Paper Concerto**, for paper percussion and orchestra (2003), is testimony to Tan's Cage-inspired penchant for new and unusual sounds.

AUSTRALIA

If composers from Asia have been successful in bridging the gap between themselves and the cultural centers of Europe and America, the same cannot yet be said for those further away. The sheer distance and remoteness of Australia from the western world has meant that our knowledge of its new music has been slow in reaching us.

Nevertheless, the music of Peter Sculthorpe (b.1929), probably Australia's most familiar export, has enjoyed continuous exposure in the west since the 60s, thanks in part to his maintaining close ties with the United States and England, where he has been both student and professor, but also to the honesty and openness of his style, which combines melodic and rhythmic borrowings from aboriginal music with elements from the traditional music of Indonesia and Japan (Sculthorpe's nearest neighbours) in a joyous, yet reverential celebration of the mystery and majesty of the Australian wilderness.

10
THE CRISIS OF CONTEMPORARY MUSIC

IT WILL BE EVIDENT BY now that the conditions prevailing at the start of the twentieth century and reinforced after the Second World War have not altered in any way. They may, in fact, be said to have become even more exaggerated. With the gradual passing of the great founding figures of modernism, and indeed the most significant trends, we are left with the uncomfortable fact that contemporary music still lacks a direction. Yet it could hardly be otherwise; fragmentation within society accelerates almost daily and reintegration is probably now unattainable. Artists are more than ever thrown back onto their own resources and, for the contemporary "classical" composer, the evident triumph of pop music must be desperately depressing. It is, though, a fact of life and gives credence to the oft-quoted view that it is popular music as a whole, rather than the music of Debussy, Stravinsky, Schoenberg and the rest, which is the true heir to the nineteenth century.

In other words, what was referred to at the beginning of this book as the split between music-as-art and music-as-entertainment, has been resolved to the benefit of the latter. This is exacerbated by the continuing lack of awareness of the existence of any contemporary "classical" music on the part of a huge proportion of the listening public. Where an awareness is evident, there is still the same old apathy; audiences have still not entirely been won over. It is obvious that education has a vital role to play in redressing the balance but there is also a growing realization that composers and organizations can raise awareness by competing for listeners in the same market-place as everyone else. Certainly there has been a noticeably more aggressive attitude to this shown in recent years, reinforced by educational work being willingly undertaken by composers, promoters and ensembles – even symphony orchestras, which we are constantly being warned are on the point of extinction.

Perhaps, in the long run, we should simply admit that music-as-art is not meant for universal consumption (what is?) and that attempts at "inclusivity" are as doomed as they are misguided. It is there as a wonderful example of what the human mind can achieve and that, if there is willing, the rewards of sharing in the experience are great indeed. However unfashionable this view may be, it will not stop the production of works of art which uphold it. Artists are not likely to abandon their vocation, even if it means lack of success and years of neglect. This means that there will always be those who plough their lonely furrow, independent of whatever appear to be the current fashionable trends.

But, ultimately, the future may rest with those whose field of enquiry is identical to Henry Cowell's "whole world of music"[38] (now a much bigger world than even he envisaged) and who have sufficient imagination to create new works which challenge our perceptions of art and at the same time give some meaning to our lives.

Notes

Notes to Part 1
1 The Beginnings
1. See, for example, Griffiths, 1978, p.7.
2. See his article, Edgard Varèse, in Cage, 1961, pp.83–4.

2 Nationalism, Folk Music, Exoticism
3. Manuel de Falla: *Claude Debussy and Spain*, in Falla, 1979, p.42.
4. Zimmermann, 1976.
5. Cowell: 'Towards Neo-Primitivism' in *Modern Music* 10 (3), quoted in Nicholls (ed.), 1997, p.8.

3 Serialism
6. In *Schoenberg, Berg, Webern; The String Quartets: A Documentary Study*, ed. Ursula v. Rauchhaupt, trans. Eugene Hartzell. Booklet accompanying the original LP recording of the quartets by the Lasalle Quartet on Deutsche Grammophon (DG 2720 029)
7. Vague tonal references may be detected, and notes 11, 12 and 1 form a B minor triad!
8. See, for example, Tomkins, 1976, pp.84–5.

4 Neo-Classicism
9. Ferruccio Busoni, *Young Classicism* in Busoni, 1957, p.21.
10. *cf.* p.19.
11. *cf.* p.50.
12. See Simpson, 1952, *passim*.

Notes to Part 2
1 A Fresh Beginning
13. The full list is given in Johnson, 1975, Appendix 2.
14. For more on this piece, see Harvey, 1975.
15. Cage, 1961, pp.71–2.
16. In **45' for a Speaker**, an experimental lecture written in 1954 and printed in Cage, 1961, p.148 et seq.

17. This piece occupies a similar position in Henze's oeuvre as does the **Folk Songs** (1964) in Berio's.
18. See p.179 for further references to this aspect of the piece.
19. Personal communication with the author, May 14, 2006.
20. James Tenney: booklet accompanying the Wergo recording of the collected Nancarrow Studies (Wergo 6907–6911). The booklet contains detailed descriptions of all the studies.

2 MINIMALISM

21. A tape loop is a length of tape with its two ends joined together. Playing the loop back on a tape recorder allows the sound recorded thereon to repeat indefinitely.
22. More accurately, modality.

3 POST-MINIMALISM

23. Hocket: a way of sharing a melodic line between two performers, one singing or playing the odd-numbered notes, the other the even-numbered ones.
24. See Hillier, 1989, *passim*.

4 RESPONSES

25. Ironically, this concept brings to mind the works of the American minimalist Tom Johnson (b.1939). In **Failing** (1975) for double bassist and **Triple Threat** (1979) for pianist, the players recite texts during their performance, detailing the difficulties of the pieces and the strong possibilities of making mistakes.
26. Richard Toop, Four Facets of 'The New Complexity', Contact, Spring 1988.

5 PIONEERS COME OF AGE

27. John Cage, Introduction to 'Lecture on Something', in Cage, 1961, p.128.
28. Morton Feldman, 'Crippled Symmetry', in Feldman, 2000, p.143.

6 OTHER RESPONSES

29. Helmut Lachenmann, in the notes to the CD recording (ECM New Series, 1789).

7 REFERENCE AND QUOTATION

30. See p.122.
31. Robin Holloway in 'What's New?', Central Independent TV Broadcast, 1988
32. *cf.* p.107 et seq.
33. *cf.* p.105.

8 OTHER CURRENTS
   34. Nicholas Maw in Griffiths, 1985.
   35. David Matthews, in the liner notes of *In the Dark Time* and *Chaconne* (NMC D067).

9 WINDS FROM THE EAST
   36. Unsuk Chin, in the liner notes to the CD recording (Deutsche Grammophon 00289 477 5118).
   37. Takemitsu's **Twelve Songs for Guitar** (1977) includes arrangements of songs by Gershwin, Arlen and the Beatles.

10 THE CRISIS OF CONTEMPORARY MUSIC
   38. Weisgall, H, 'The Music of Henry Cowell', in *Musical Quarterly* 45 (4), 1959, p.498.

Suggested Further Reading

Burt, Peter. *The Music of Tōru Takemitsu*. Cambridge: Cambridge University Press, 2001.
Busoni, Ferruccio. *The Essence of Music*. London: Rockliff, 1957.
Cage, John. *Silence*. Cambridge, Mass and London: MIT Press, 1961.
De Falla, Manuel. *On Music and Musicians*. London and Boston: Marion Boyars,1979.
Feldman, Morton. *Give my Regards to 8th Street (Collected Writings of Morton Feldman)*. Cambridge, Mass: Exact Change, 2000.
Griffiths, Paul. *A Concise History of Modern Music*. London: Thames & Hudson, 1978.
Griffiths, Paul. *Modern Music and After*. New York: Oxford University Press, 1995.
Griffiths, Paul. *New Sounds, New Personalities; British Composers of the 1980s*. London: Faber Music Ltd, 1985.
Hall, Michael. *Harrison Birtwistle*. London: Robson, 1984.
Harvey, Jonathan. *The Music of Stockhausen*. London: Faber & Faber, 1975.
Hillier, Paul. *Arvo Pärt*. New York: Oxford University Press, 1997.
Johnson, Robert Sherlaw. *Messiaen*. London: J.M.Dent & Sons, 1975
Nicholls, David, ed. *The Whole World of Music; A Henry Cowell Symposium*. Amsterdam: Harwood Academic Publishers, 1997.
Potter, Keith. *Four Musical Minimalists*. Cambridge University Press, 2000.
Pritchett, James. *The Music of John Cage*. Cambridge: Cambridge University Press, 1993.

Simpson, Robert. *Carl Nielsen, Symphonist*. London: J.M.Dent & Sons, 1952; 2nd rev. edn London & New York: Kahn & Averill, 1979; p/b edn, London: Kahn & Averill, 1986.

Strickland, Edward. *American Composers*. Bloomington & Indianapolis: Indiana University Press, 1987.

Tomkins, Calvin. *The Bride & the Bachelors; Five Masters of the Avant-Garde*. New York: The Viking Press, 1965; p/b edn Penguin Books, 1976.

Zimmermann, Walter. *Desert Plants; Conversations with 23 American Musicians*. Vancouver: Walter Zimmermann & A.R.C. Publications, 1976.

INDEX

A
Adams, John 147, 199
Added resonance 92, 159
Adès, Thomas 198, 199
Aeschylus 74
African music 140
Albéniz, Isaac 47
Aleatoricism 118, 119
Ambient 148, 149
AMM 123
Anderson, Julian 198, 199
Andriessen, Louis 150
Apollinaire, Guillaume 75
Ashley, Robert 123
Atonality 24, 55, 59, 60, 89
Auric, Georges 73

B
Babbitt, Milton 62, 96
Bach, J.S. 60, 67, 71, 78, 169, 188
Bainbridge, Simon 189
Ballets Russes 30
Bang on a Can 149
Barrett, Richard 157
Barry, Gerald 183, 200
Bartók, Béla 15, 39, 40, 43, 44, 45, 51, 53, 56, 133, 179, 184
Baudelaire, Charles 22
Bax, Arnold 46
Bayle, François 101
BBC Philharmonic Orchestra 169
Beckett, Samuel 180
Beethoven, Ludwig van 71, 121, 177, 192
Behrman, David 123

Bekker, Paul 67
Benjamin, George 160, 161, 162, 202
Bennett, Richard Rodney 190
Berberian, Cathy 104, 107
Berg, Alban 24, 25, 26, 60, 61, 94, 190, 193
Berio, Luciano 104, 107, 108, 119, 166, 167, 174, 179, 181
Berkeley, Lennox 46
Berners, Lord 126
Bernstein, Leonard 83
Birtwistle, Harrison 107, 108, 109, 121
Bitonality 17, 31, 55, 69
Black Mountain College, North Carolina 105, 112
Boogie-woogie 131
Boulanger, Nadia 54, 82
Boulez, Pierre 95, 96, 97, 98, 109, 117, 118, 156, 159, 160, 166, 167, 171, 174, 190, 192, 199
Bowie, David 143
Brahms, Johannes 25, 61, 179
Branca, Glenn 150
Brecht, George 79, 135
Bridge, Frank 43, 45
Britten, Benjamin 15, 43, 77, 78, 124, 193, 194, 200
Brown, Earle 112, 114, 116
Browning, Robert 55
Bruckner, Anton 192
Brussels World Fair 102
Bryars, Gavin 126
Busoni, Ferruccio 35, 67, 100, 126
Butterworth, George 45

C

Cage, John 15, 36, 63, 64, 89, 105, 107, 110, 111, 112, 116, 117, 118, 119, 122, 124, 125, 127, 128, 135, 154, 158, 163, 164, 165, 202, 205
Cardew, Cornelius 118, 124, 135
Carter, Elliott 155, 199
Chabrier, Emmanuel 20, 75, 178
Chance 65, 110, 111, 112, 116
Charleston 50
Chatham, Rhys 150
Chávez, Carlos 52
Chin, Unsuk 201, 202
Chopin, Fryderyk 179
Claudel, Paul 52
Cobbett, W.W. 43
Cocteau, Jean 73, 74
Confucius 124
Copland, Aaron 81, 82, 83
Cowell, Henry 55, 56, 63, 127, 208
Craft, Robert 156
Cunningham, Merce 105, 112

D

Dada 135
Dallapiccola, Luigi 95, 119
Dankworth, John 189
Darmstadt 95, 103, 110, 117, 119, 154, 156, 171, 199, 201
Daugherty, Michael 185
Davies, Peter Maxwell 107, 108, 109, 168, 169, 182
Davis, Miles 189
Debussy, Claude 20, 21, 22, 23, 28, 29, 34, 48, 49, 50, 57, 68, 69, 90, 132, 162, 190, 203, 207
Dench, Chris 157, 158

Developing variation 25
Diaghilev, Sergei 30, 70
Dillon, James 157
Drone 33, 136, 137
Duchamp, Marcel 135
Durey, Louis 73

E

Eckhart, Meister 116
Eimert, Herbert 102
Electro-acoustic music 102, 103, 106
Electronic music 37, 102, 132, 134
Elgar, Edward 43, 46
Eno, Brian 125, 143, 149
Evans, Gil 189
Exoticism 51
Experimental music 125, 137
Expressionism 28, 67, 122
Extended techniques 53, 134, 157

F

Falla, Manuel de 47, 48
Fauré, Gabriel 19, 45, 69
Feldman, Morton 112, 114, 115, 116, 125, 163, 164, 171, 175
Ferneyhough, Brian 157, 158, 160
Ferrari, Luc 101
Ferroud, Pierre-Octave 75
Finnissy, Michael 157
Fires of London 108, 169
First World War 28, 49, 68
Fluxus 105, 135, 202
Fox, Christopher 198, 199
Franck, César 43
French Radio (R.T.F.) 100, 101
French Revolution 16
Freud, Sigmund 18

Furrer, Beat 174
Futurists 35, 89

G

Gamelan 49, 75, 128, 129, 140
Gebrauchsmusik 76, 83, 197
Gentle Fire 123
George, Stefan 25
German West Radio (WDR) 102
Gershwin, George 51, 83
Ginastera, Alberto 52
Glass, Philip 126, 138, 141, 142, 154
Goehr, Alexander 109
Goodman, Benny 82
Gordon, Michael 148, 149
Górecki, Henryk 153
Grainger, Percy 126
Granados, Enrique 47
Gregorian chant 90, 152
Grisey, Gérard 159
Grünewald, Mathias 78

H

Handel, George Frideric 42, 184
Harrison, Lou 127, 128
Harris, Roy 83
Harvey, Jonathan 159
Haydn, Joseph 71
Henry, Pierre 101
Henze, Hans Werner 119, 121, 124, 179
Herman, Woody 50
Hindemith, Paul 49, 76, 77, 78
Hip-hop 148
Holloway, Robin 180
Holst, Gustav 43, 45
Honegger, Arthur 73, 74

Hosokawa, Toshio 204
House 148
Hymns Ancient and Modern 126

I

I Ching 110, 111, 165
Ichiyanagi, Toshi 202
Impressionism 67, 69
Improvisation 123, 136, 137
Indeterminacy 116, 117, 118, 119
Indian music 90, 91, 141
Integral serialism 96, 97, 98, 99, 103, 117
Intermodulation 123
IRCAM 159, 160, 166
Isorhythm 109
Ives, Charles 54, 55, 75, 83, 127, 155, 158, 177, 178, 199
Ives, George 54

J

Janáček, Leoš 47, 144
Jazz 33, 50, 51, 75, 82, 83, 123, 126, 130, 137, 138, 144, 147, 148, 149, 150, 174, 178, 183, 188, 189, 190, 193, 203
Johnson, Tom 210
Jones, Spike 182
Joplin, Scott 50
Joyce, James 104, 165, 180, 204
Jung, Carl 18

K

Kagel, Mauricio 105, 107, 108, 118, 183, 200
Klangfarbenmelodie 29
Klee, Paul 133
Knussen, Oliver 198, 199

Korot, Beryl 144
Kosugi, Takehisa 202

L
Lachenmann, Helmut 171, 173
Lang, David 149
Leitmotiv 25
Les Six 73
Ligeti, György 131, 132, 158
Liszt, Franz 17, 43
Live electronic music 106
London Symphony Orchestra 83
Lucier, Alvin 122, 123
Lutosławski, Witold 118

M
MacMillan, James 187
Maderna, Bruno 95, 104
Magic squares 110, 168
Mahler, Gustav 17, 18, 24, 26, 75, 179, 193
Mallarmé, Stéphane 22, 69, 167
Marinetti, Filippo 35
Martinů, Bohuslav 50
Martland, Steve 150
Mathias, William 193
Matthews, Colin 198, 199
Matthews, David 193, 197, 199
Maw, Nicholas 192
Maxwell Davies, Peter. *See* Davies, Peter Maxwell
McCabe, John 193
Mendelssohn, Felix 43
Messiaen, Olivier 15, 90, 91, 92, 94, 95, 96, 100, 109, 141, 159, 160, 162, 187, 202, 203
Metheny, Pat 144
Metric modulation 156

Micro-polyphony 133, 158
Microtone 157, 172
Milhaud, Darius 21, 50, 51, 52, 73, 74, 82
Minimalism 133, 135
Modes of limited transposition 90
Mozart, Wolfgang Amadeus 67, 68, 71, 75, 119, 121
Multiphonics 134, 157
Mumma, Gordon 123
Murail, Tristan 159, 160
Musica Elettronica Viva 123
Musique concrète 100, 102

N
Nancarrow, Conlon 130, 131, 133, 158
Nath, Pandit Pran 137
Nationalism 16, 39, 52, 67
Neo-classicism 67, 73, 75, 89
Neue Sachlichkeit 68
New Complexity 156, 157
Nielsen, Carl 84, 85, 192, 197
Nono, Luigi 95, 124, 171
Non-retrogradable rhythm 92
Nyman, Michael 126

O
Oriental music 22, 137
Owen, Wilfred 194

P
Paik, Nam June 122
Paris Conservatoire 94
Paris Exposition (1889) 22, 49
Parmegiani, Bernard 101
Pärt, Arvo 151, 152, 153
Partch, Harry 127, 128, 129

Pears, Peter 77
Penderecki, Krzysztof 133, 153, 168
Pentatonic 22, 23
Pergolesi, Giovanni Batista 70
Perotin 152
Phasing 138, 139, 140
Pianola 130
Piazzolla, Astor 53
Pierrot Players 108
Pintscher, Matthias 174
Plainchant 19, 21, 92, 109
Player piano 130
Poe, Edgar Allan 22
Pollock, Jackson 112
Polystylism 51, 57, 75
Polystylistics 181
Polytonality 74
Popular music 18, 21, 49, 51, 75, 103
Porter, Cole 190
Portsmouth Sinfonia 125
Poulenc, Francis 21, 73, 74, 75, 177, 181
Pousseur, Henri 95
Prepared piano 64, 128, 152
Progressive tonality 84
Prokofiev, Sergei 28, 81
Purcell, Henry 42

Q
Quartal harmony 18, 23
Quilter, Roger 45

R
Rachmaninov, Sergei 126
Ragtime 21, 33, 50
Rakha, Allah 141
Rauschenberg, Robert 112
Ravel, Maurice 16, 21, 48, 49, 50, 68, 179
Red Poppies 149
Reggio, Godfrey 143
Reich, Steve 137, 138, 139, 140, 141, 143, 144, 145, 153, 154
Revueltas, Silvestre 52
Rihm, Wolfgang 173, 174
Riley, Terry 137
Rimsky-Korsakov, Nikolai 30
Rock 148
Rodney Bennett, Richard.
    See Bennett, Richard Rodney
Romanticism 17, 19, 21, 24, 34, 67
Rossini, Gioachino 178, 179
Royal Manchester College of Music 109
Royal Northern College of Music 109
Ruders, Poul 190, 199
Russolo, Luigi 35
Rzewski, Frederic 123, 124

S
Saariaho, Kaija 160, 172
Saint-Saëns, Camille 75
Satie, Erik 19, 20, 22, 24, 30, 31, 49, 73, 75, 83, 125, 126, 165
Saunders, Rebecca 172
Saxton, Robert 198
Scelsi, Giacinto 172, 173
Schaeffer, Pierre 101
Schnittke, Alfred 75, 180
Schoenberg, Arnold 24, 25, 27, 28, 59, 60, 61, 62, 63, 69, 73, 74, 89, 94, 96, 108, 109, 190, 207
Schola Cantorum 19

Schuller, Gunther 189
Schumann, Robert 45
Scodanibbio, Stefano 167
Scottish Chamber Orchestra 169
Scratch Orchestra 124, 125, 135
Scriabin, Alexander 27
Sculthorpe, Peter 205
Second Viennese School 24, 94
Second World War 37, 90, 144, 179, 181, 207
Serialism 60, 62, 63, 73, 89, 94, 119, 120
Shankar, Ravi 141
Sharngadeva 91
Shostakovich, Dmitri 49, 80, 178, 179, 180, 192, 204
Sibelius, Jean 84, 169
Simpson, Robert 192
Skempton, Howard 125
Socrates 21
Sonic Arts Group 123
Sonic Arts Union 123
Sprechgesang 28, 107, 108
Stockhausen, Karlheinz 56, 95, 97, 98, 99, 102, 103, 106, 109, 118, 123, 124, 132, 164, 165, 171
Strauss, Richard 17, 18
Stravinsky, Igor 28, 30, 32, 33, 39, 40, 50, 54, 70, 71, 73, 75, 82, 89, 91, 109, 120, 121, 150, 156, 168, 184, 193, 199, 207
Studio di Fonologia Musicale 104
Surrealism 133
Szymanowski, Karol 28

T

Tailleferre, Germaine 73
Takemitsu, Tōru 202, 203, 204
Tan Dun 204
Tavener, John 153
Tchaikovsky, Piotr 75, 184
Techno 148
Tharp, Twyla 143
Thomson, Virgil 83
Thoreau, Henry David 55
Tibetan Buddhism 173
Tintinnabuli 153
Tippett, Michael 78, 79, 124, 155, 193
Tone cluster 56
Torke, Michael 148
Tudor, David 105, 112
Turnage, Mark-Anthony 188, 189

V

Varèse, Edgard 35, 36, 64, 100, 102, 158, 171
Vaughan Williams, Ralph 43, 44, 45, 51, 53
Villa-Lobos, Heitor 52
Vischer, Antoinette 133

W

Wagner, Richard 17, 19, 25, 122, 166, 178, 179
Walton, William 43, 49
Webern, Anton 15, 16, 24, 27, 29, 59, 60, 61, 62, 89, 94, 95, 109, 156
Weill, Kurt 15, 79
Weimar Republic 80
Weir, Judith 184, 185
West German Radio (WDR) 102, 132
White, John 153
Whole tone scale 22, 23, 60

Wilson, Robert 142
Wolfe, Julia 149
Wolff, Christian 112, 113, 116, 124
Woolf, Virginia 180

X
Xenakis, Iannis 158

Y
Young, LaMonte 135, 136
Yun, Isang 201, 202, 204

Z
Zen Buddhism 65, 110, 116, 135, 203
Zimmermann, Walter 54

Made in the USA
Monee, IL
18 May 2020